SRI RAMAKRISHNA

BY

SWAMI NIKHILĀNANDA

SRI RAMAKRISHNA MATH
MYLAPORE :: MADRAS - 4

Published by
The President
Sri Ramakrishna Math
Mylapore, Chennai-4

X-2M 3C-5-2004
ISBN 81-7120-971-8

Printed in India at
Sri Ramakrishna Math Printing Press
Mylapore, Chennai-4

FOREWORD

Sri Ramakrishna forms the Preface of **The Gospel of Sri Ramakrishna**, published in 1942 by the Ramakrishna Vivekananda Centre of New York, U.S.A. It contains a short biography of the Prophet of modern India based mainly upon the Life of Sri Ramakrishna, a publication of the Advaita Ashrama, Mayavati. Also included are short explanations of several systems of Indian religious thought associated with Sri Ramakrishna's spiritual disciplines and experiences.

The last part of the book, entitled "After the Passing Away," gives a picture of the daily life of Sri Ramakrishna's disciples after his death and reveals the ascetic background of the Ramakrishna Mission.

Sri Ramakrishna is becoming recognized today as the great manifestation of Divinity in modern times. His varied spiritual experiences, his harmonization of different faiths and his demonstration of the complete triumph of man over his lower nature mark him as a unique figure in the spiritual history of the world. Sri Ramakrishna is a fact of history, the first God-man who was photographed and whose words were recorded with stenographic precision.

The advent of Sri Ramakrishna represents the dawn of a new age in India. The movement for the freedom of the Indian people, whatever may have been its later development, originated at Dakshineswar. The spiritual yearning cherished by three hundred millions of Hindus for the past three thousand years found its fulfilment in the realizations of Sri Ramakrishna. And Swami Vivekananda applied his Master's teachings for the solution of the many problems by which the world is beset today, brought to a focus by science and technology. It is to the universal teachings of Sri Ramakrishna that people everywhere are eagerly looking, often unknowingly, for the light that will destroy their present doubt and confusion and promote peace and goodwill among all.

NIKHILANANDA

Ramakrishna—Vivekananda Centre
NEW YORK
JANUARY 1, 1953

CONTENTS

EARLY YEARS 1

Boyhood-Coming to Calcutta-Bread winning education.

PRIEST AT DAKSHINESWAR TEMPLE ...

Siva-Radhakanta-Kali-Sri Ramakrishna as a Priest-The first vision of Kali.

GOD - INTOXICATED STATE 21

Haladhari-Marriage and after-The Brahmani-Tantra-Vaishnava disciplines-Ramlala-In communion with the divine beloved - Vedanta - Totapuri - Kali and maya-Totapuri's lesson.

THE MASTER IN THE MAKING 53

Islam-Christianity-Attitude towards different religions-Pilgrimage-Relation with his wife—The 'Ego' of the Master-Summary of the Master's spiritual experiences-Brahmo Samaj - Arya Samaj - Keshavchandra Sen-Other Brahmo leaders.

COMING OF DISCIPLES 77

The Master's method of teaching-Householder devotees-Future monks-Ram and Monomohan-Surendra-Kedar-Harish-Bhavanath-Balaram Bose-Mahendra or 'M'-Nag Mahashay-Girish Ghosh-Purna-Mahimacharan and Pratap Hazra-Some noted men-Kristodas Pal-Monastic disciples-Latu-Rakhal-The elder Gopal.

NARENDRANATH AND OTHER DISCIPLES ... 94

Tarak-Baburam-Niranjan-Jogindra-Sashi and Sarat-Harinath - Gangadhar - Hariprasanna - Kali - Subodh-Sarada-Woman devotees-Gopal Ma-The march of events-Injury to the Master's arm.

ILLNESS AND MAHASAMADHI 112

Shyampukur-Last days at Kashipur-Mahasamadhi.

AFTER THE PASSING AWAY 124

CHAPTER I

EARLY YEARS

$\mathscr{S}$RI RAMAKRISHNA, the God-man of modern India, was born at Kāmārpukur. This village in the Hooghly District preserved during the last century the idyllic simplicity of the rural areas of Bengal. Situated far from the railway, it was untouched by the glamour of the city. It contained rice-fields, tall palms, royal banyans, a few lakes and two cremation grounds. South of the village a stream took its leisurely course. A mango orchard dedicated by a neighbouring zemindar to the public use was frequented by the boys for their noonday sports. A highway passed through the village to the great temple of Jagannāth at Purī, and the villagers, most of whom were farmers and craftsmen, entertained many passing holy men and pilgrims. The dull round of the rural life was broken by lively festivals, the observance of sacred days, religious singing, and other innocent pleasures.

About his parents Sri Ramakrishna once said: " My mother was the personification of rectitude and gentleness. She did not know much about the ways of the world; innocent of the art of concealment, she would say what was in her mind. People loved her for her open-heartedness. My father, an orthodox brāhmin, never accepted gifts from the sudras. He spent much of his time in worship and meditation, and in repeating God's name and chanting His glories. Whenever in his daily prayers he invoked the goddess Gāyatri, his chest flushed and tears rolled down his cheeks. He spent his leisure hours making garlands for the family deity, Raghuvīr."

Khudiram Chattopādhyāya and Chandrā Devī, the parents of Sri Ramakrishna, were married in 1799. At that time Khudiram was living in his ancestral village of Dereypore, not far from Kāmārpukur. Their first son, Ramkumar, was born in 1805, and their first daughter, Kātyāyanī, in 1810. In 1814 Khudiram was ordered by his landlord to bear false witness in court against a neighbour. When he refused to do so, the landlord brought a false case against him and deprived him of his ancestral property. Thus dispossessed, he arrived, at the invitation of another landlord, in the quiet village of Kāmārpukur, where he was given a dwelling and about an acre of fertile land. The crops from this little property were enough to meet his family's simple needs. Here he lived in simplicity, dignity, and contentment.

Ten years after his coming to Kāmārpukur, Khudiram made a pilgrimage on foot to Rāmeswar, at the southern extremity of India. Two years later was born his second son, whom he named Rāmeswar. Again in 1835, at the age of sixty, he made a pilgrimage, this time to Gayā. Here, from ancient times, Hindus have come from the four corners of India to discharge their duties to their departed ancestors by offering them food and drink at the sacred footprint of the Lord Vishnu. At this holy place Khudiram had a dream in which the Lord Vishnu promised to be born as his son. And Chandrā Devī, too, in front of the Siva temple at Kāmārpukur, had a vision indicating the birth of a divine child. Upon his return, the husband found that she had conceived.

It was on February 18, 1836, that the child, to be known afterwards as Ramakrishna, was born. In memory of the dream at Gayā he was given the name of Gadādhar, the "Bearer of the Mace", an epithet of Vishnu. Three years later a little sister was born.

BOYHOOD

Gadādhar grew up into a healthy and restless boy, full of fun and sweet mischief. He was intelligent and precocious and endowed with a prodigious memory. On his father's lap he learnt by heart the names of his ancestors and the hymns to the gods and goddesses, and at the village school he was taught to read and write. But his greatest delight was to listen to recitations of stories from Hindu mythology and the epics. These he would afterwards recount from memory, to the great joy of the villagers. Painting he enjoyed; the art of moulding images of the gods and goddesses he learnt from the potters. But arithmetic was his great aversion.

At the age of six or seven Gadādhar had his first experience of spiritual ecstasy. One day in June or July, when he was walking along a narrow path between paddy-fields, eating the puffed rice that he carried in a basket, he looked up at the sky and saw a beautiful, dark thunder-cloud. As it spread, rapidly enveloping the whole sky, a flight of snow-white cranes passed in front of it. The beauty of the contrast overwhelmed the boy. He fell to the ground, unconscious, and the puffed rice went in all directions. Some villagers found him and carried him home in their arms. Gadādhar said later that in that state he had experienced an indescribable joy.

Gadādhar was seven years old when his father died. This incident profoundly affected him. For the first time the boy realized that life on earth was impermanent. Unobserved by others, he began to slip into the mango orchard or into one of the cremation grounds, and he spent hours absorbed in his own thoughts. He also became more helpful to his mother in the discharge of her household duties. He gave more attention to reading and hearing the religious stories recorded in the Purānas. And he became interested in the wandering monks and pious pilgrims who would stop at Kāmārpukur on their way to Puri. These holy men, the custodians of India's spiritual heritage and the living witnesses of the ideal of renunciation of the world and all-absorbing love of God, entertained the little boy with stories from the Hindu epics, stories of saints and prophets, and also stories of their own adventures. He, on his part, fetched their water and fuel and served them in various ways. Meanwhile, he was observing their meditation and worship.

At the age of nine Gadādhar was invested with the sacred thread. This ceremony conferred upon him the privileges of his brāhmin lineage, including the worship of the family deity, Raghuvir, and imposed upon him the many strict disciplines of a brāhmin's life. During the ceremony of investiture he shocked his relatives by accepting a meal cooked by his nurse, a sudra woman. His father would never have dreamt of doing such a thing. But in a playful mood Gadādhar had once promised this woman that he would eat her food, and now he fulfilled his plighted word. The woman had piety and religious sincerity, and these were more important to the boy than the conventions of society.

Gadādhar was now permitted to worship Raghuvir. Thus began his first training in meditation. He so gave his heart and soul to the worship that the stone image very soon appeared to him as the living Lord of the universe. His tendency to lose himself in contemplation was first noticed at this time. Behind his boyish light-heartedness was seen a deepening of his spiritual nature.

About this time, on the S'ivarātri night, consecrated to the worship of S'iva, a dramatic performance was arranged. The principal actor, who was to play the part of S'iva, suddenly fell ill, and Gadādhar was persuaded to act in his place. While friends were dressing him for the role of S'iva—smearing his body with ashes, matting his locks, placing a trident in his hand and a string of rudrāksha beads around his neck—the boy appeared to become absent-minded. He approached the stage with slow and measured step, supported by his friends. He looked the living image of S'iva. The audience loudly applauded what it took to be his skill as an actor, but it was soon discovered that he was really lost in meditation. His countenance was radiant and tears flowed from his eyes. He was lost to the outer world. The effect of this scene on the audience was tremendous. The people felt blessed as by a vision of S'iva Himself. The performance had to be stopped, and the boy's mood lasted till the following morning.

Gadādhar himself now organized a dramatic company with his young friends. The stage was set in the mango orchard. The themes were selected from the stories of the *Ramayana* and the *Mahabharata*. Gadādhar knew by heart almost all the roles, having heard them from professional actors. His favourite theme was the Vrindāvan episode of Krishna's life, depicting those exquisite love-stories of Krishna and the milkmaids and the cowherd-boys. Gadādhar would play the parts of Rādhā or Krishna and would often lose himself in the character he was portraying. His natural feminine grace heightened the dramatic effect. The mango-orchard would ring with the loud kirtan of the boys. Lost in song and merry-making, Gadādhar became indifferent to the routine of school.

In 1849 Ramkumar, the eldest son, went to Calcutta to improve the financial condition of the family.

Gadādhar was on the threshold of youth. He had become the pet of the women of the village. They loved to hear him talk, sing, or recite from the holy books. They enjoyed his knack of imitating voices. Their woman's instinct recognized the innate purity and guilelessness of this boy of clear skin, flowing hair, beaming eyes, smiling face, and inexhaustible fun.

The pious elderly women looked upon him as Gopāla, the baby Krishna, and the younger ones saw in him the youthful Krishna of Vrindāvan. He himself so idealized the love of the gopis for Krishna that he sometimes yearned to be born as a woman, if he must be born again, in order to be able to love Sri Krishna with all his heart and soul.

COMING TO CALCUTTA

At the age of sixteen Gadādhar was summoned to Calcutta by his elder brother Ramkumar, who wished assistance in his priestly duties. Ramkumar had opened a Sanskrit academy to supplement his income, and it was his intention gradually to turn his younger brother's mind to education. Gadādhar applied himself heart and soul to his new duty as family priest to a number of Calcutta families. His worship was very different from that of the professional priests. He spent hours decorating the images and singing hymns and devotional songs; he performed with love the other duties of his office. People were impressed with his ardour. But to his studies he paid scant attention.

Ramkumar did not at first oppose the ways of his temperamental brother. He wanted Gadādhar to become used to the conditions of city life. But one day he decided to warn the boy about his indifference to the world. After all, in the near future Gadādhar must, as a householder, earn his livelihood through the performance of his brāhminical duties; and these required a thorough knowledge of Hindu law, astrology, and kindred subjects. He gently admonished Gadādhar and asked him to pay more attention to his studies. But the boy replied spiritedly: "Brother, what shall I do with a mere bread-winning education? I would rather acquire that wisdom which will illumine my heart and give me satisfaction for ever."

BREAD-WINNING EDUCATION

The anguish of the inner soul of India found expression through these passionate words of the young Gadādhar. For what did his unsophisticated eyes see around him in Calcutta, at that time the metropolis of India and the centre of modern culture and learning? Greed and lust held sway in the higher levels of society, and the occasional religious practices were merely outer forms from which the soul had long ago departed. Gadādhar had never seen anything like this at Kāmārpukur among the simple and pious villagers. The sādhus and wandering monks whom he had served in his boyhood had revealed to him an altogether different India. He had been impressed by their devotion and purity, their self-control and renunciation. He had learnt from them and from his own intuition that the ideal of life as taught by the ancient sages of India was the realization of God.

When Ramkumar reprimanded Gadādhar for neglecting a "bread-wining education," the inner voice of the boy reminded him that the legacy of his ancestors—the legacy of Rama, Krishna, Buddha, S'ankara, Ramanuja, Chaitanya—was not worldly security but the knowledge of God. And these noble sages were the true representatives of Hindu society. Each of them was seated, as it were, on the crest of the wave that followed each successive trough in the tumultuous course of Indian national life. All demonstrated that the life current of India is spirituality. This truth was revealed to Gadādhar through that inner vision which scans past and future in one sweep, unobstructed by the barriers of time and space. But he was unaware of the history of the profound change that had taken place in the land of his birth during the previous one hundred years.

Hindu society during the eighteenth century had been passing through a period of decadence. It was the twilight of the

Mussalmān rule. There were anarchy and confusion in all spheres. Superstitious practices dominated the religious life of the people. Rites and rituals passed for the essence of spirituality. Greedy priests became the custodians of heaven. True philosophy was supplanted by dogmatic opinions. The pundits took delight in vain polemics.

In 1757 English traders laid the foundation of British rule in India. Gradually the Government was systematized and lawlessness suppressed. The Hindus were much impressed by the military power and political acumen of the new rulers. In the wake of the merchants came the English educators, and social reformers, and Christian missionaries—all bearing a culture completely alien to the Hindu mind. In different parts of the country educational institutions were set up and Christian churches established. Hindu young men were offered the heady wine of the western culture of the late eighteenth and early nineteenth centuries, and they drank it to the very dregs.

The first effect of the draught on the educated Hindus was a complete effacement from their minds of the time-honoured beliefs and traditions of Hindu society. They came to believe that there was no transcendental truth. The world perceived by the senses was all that existed. God and religion were illusions of the untutored mind. True knowledge could be derived only from the analysis of nature. So atheism and agnosticism became the fashion of the day. The youth of India, taught in English schools, took malicious delight in openly breaking the customs and traditions of their society. They would do away with the caste-system and remove the discriminatory laws about food. Social reform, the spread of secular education, widow-remarriage, abolition of early marriage—they considered these the panacea for the degenerate condition of Hindu society.

The Christian missionaries gave the finishing touch to the process of transformation. They ridiculed as relics of a barbarous age, the images and rituals of the Hindu religion. They tried to persuade India that the teachings of her saints and seers were the cause of her downfall, that her Vedas, Purānas, and other scriptures were filled with superstition. Christianity, they maintained, had given the white races position and power in this world and assurance of happiness in the next; therefore Christianity was the best of all religions. Many intelligent young Hindus became converted. The man in the street was confused. The majority of the educated grew materialistic in their mental outlook. Everyone living near Calcutta or the other strongholds of western culture, even those who attempted to cling to the orthodox traditions of Hindu society, became infected by the new uncertainties and the new beliefs.

But the soul of India was to be resuscitated through a spiritual awakening. We hear the first call of this renaissance in the spirited retort of the young Gadādhar: "Brother, what shall I do with a mere bread-winning education?"

Ramkumar could hardly understand the import of his young brother's reply. He described in bright colours the happy and easy life of scholars in Calcutta society. But Gadādhar intuitively felt that the scholars, to use one of his own vivid illustrations, were like so many vultures, soaring high on the wings of their uninspired intellect, with their eyes fixed on the charnel-pit of greed and lust. So he stood firm . and Ramkumar had to give way.

CHAPTER II

PRIEST AT DAKSHINESWAR TEMPLE

AT that time there lived in Calcutta a rich widow named Rānī Rāsmani, belonging to the sudra caste, and known far and wide not only for her business ability, courage, and intelligence, but also for her largeness of heart, piety and devotion to God. She was assisted in the management of her vast property by her son-in-law Mathuramohan.

In 1847 the Rānī purchased twenty acres of land at Dakshineswar, a village about four miles north of Calcutta. Here she created a temple garden and constructed several temples. Her Ishta, or chosen ideal, was the divine Mother, Kāli.

The temple-garden stands directly on the east bank of the Ganges. The northern section of the land and a portion to the east contain an orchard, flower-gardens, and two small reservoirs. The southern section is paved with brick and mortar. The visitor arriving by boat ascends the steps of an imposing bathing-ghāt which leads to the chāndni, a roofed terrace, on either side of which stand in a row six temples of S'iva. East of the terrace and the S'iva temples is a large court, paved, rectangular in shape, and running north and south. Two temples stand in the centre of this court, the larger one, to the south and facing south, being dedicated to Kāli, and the smaller one, facing the Ganges, to Rādhākānta, that is, Krishna, the consort of Rādhā. Nine domes with spires surmount the temple of Kāli, and before it stands the spacious nātmandir, or music-hall, the terrace of which is supported by stately pillars. At the north-west and south-west corners of the temple-compound are two *nahavats*, or music-towers, from which music flows at different times of day, especially at sun-up, noon, and sun-down, when the worship is

performed in the temples.   Three sides of the paved courtyard—
all except the west—are lined with rooms set apart for kitchens,
store-rooms, dining rooms, and quarters for the temple staff and
guests. The chamber in the north-west angle, just beyond the last
of the S'iva temples, is of special interest to us ; for here Sri
Ramakrishna was to spend a considerable part of his life.   To the
west of this chamber is a semicircular porch overlooking the river.
In front of the porch runs a foot-path, north and south, and
beyond the path is a large garden and, below the garden, the
Ganges.   The orchard to the north of the buildings contains the
Panchavati, the banyan, and the bel-tree, associated with Sri
Ramakrishna's spiritual practices.   Outside and to the north of
the temple-compound proper is the *kuthi*, or bungalow, used by
members of Rānī Rāsmani's family visiting the garden. And north
of the temple-garden, separated from it by a high wall, is a
powder-magazine belonging to the British Government.

S'IVA

In the twelve S'iva temples are installed the emblems of the
great God of renunciation in His various aspects, worshipped
daily with proper rites. S'iva requires few articles of worship.
White flowers and bel-leaves and a little Ganges water offered
with devotion are enough to satisfy the benign Deity and win
from Him the boon of liberation.

RĀDHĀKĀNTA

The temple of Rādhākānta, also known as the temple of
Vishnu, contains the images of Rādhā and Krishna, the symbol
of union with God through ecstatic love. The two images stand
on a pedestal facing the west. The floor is paved with marble.
From the ceiling of the porch hang chandeliers protected from
dust by coverings of red cloth. Canvas screens shield the
images from the rays of the setting sun.   Close to the threshold

of the inner shrine is a small brass cup containing holy water. Devoted visitors reverently drink a few drops from the vessel.

KĀLI

The main temple is dedicated to Kāli, the divine Mother, here worshipped as Bhavatārini, the saviour of the universe. The floor of this temple also is paved with marble. The basalt image of the Mother, dressed in gorgeous gold brocade, stands on a white marble image of the prostrate body of Her divine consort, Siva, the symbol of the Absolute. On the feet of the goddess are, among other ornaments, anklets of gold. Her arms are decked with jewelled ornaments of gold. She wears necklaces of gold and pearls, a golden garland of human heads, and a girdle of human arms. She wears a golden crown, golden ear-rings, and a golden nose-ring with a pearl-drop. She has four arms. The lower left hand holds a severed human head and the upper grips a blood-stained sabre. One right hand offers boons to Her children; the other allays their fear. The majesty of Her posture can hardly be described. It combines the terror of destruction with the reassurance of motherly tenderness. For She is the cosmic Power, the totality of the universe, a glorious harmony of the pairs of opposites. She deals out death, as She creates and preserves. She has three eyes, the third being the symbol of divine wisdom; they strike dismay into the wicked, yet pour out affection for Her devotees.

The whole symbolic world is represented in the temple garden—the trinity of the nature Mother (Kāli), the Absolute (S'iva), and love (Rādhākānta), the arch spanning heaven and earth. The terrific goddess of the Tantra, the soul-enthralling flute-player of the *Bhāgavata*, and the self-absorbed Absolute of the Vedas live together, creating the greatest synthesis of religions. All aspects of reality are represented there. But of this divine household, Kāli is the pivot, the sovereign mistress. She is Prakriti, the Procreatrix, Nature, the Destroyer, the Creator. Nay, She is something greater and deeper still for those who have eyes to see. She is the universal Mother, "my Mother", as Ramakrishna would say, "the all-powerful, who reveals Herself to Her children under different aspects and divine Incarnations, the visible God, who leads the elect to the invisible Reality; and if it so pleases Her, She takes away the last trace of ego from created beings and merges it in the consciousness of the Absolute, the undifferentiated God. Through Her grace "the finite ego loses itself in the illimitable ego—Ātman—Brahman".[1]

Rānī Rāsmani spent a fortune for the construction of the temple-garden and another fortune for its dedication ceremony, which took place on May 31, 1855.

Sri Ramakrishna—henceforth we shall call Gadādhar by this familiar name[2]—came to the temple-garden with his elder brother Ramkumar, who was appointed priest of the Kāli temple. Sri Ramakrishna did not at first approve of Ramkumar's working for the sudra Rāsmani. The example of their orthodox father was still fresh in Sri Ramakrishna's mind. He objected also to the eating of the cooked offerings of the temple, since, according to orthodox Hindu custom, such food can be offered to the Deity only in the house of a brāhmin. But the holy atmosphere of the temple grounds, the solitude of the surrounding wood, the loving care of his brother, the respect shown him by Rānī Rāsmani and Mathur Babu, the living presence of the goddess Kāli in the temple, and, above all, the proximity of the sacred Ganges, which

---

[1] Romain Rolland, *Prophets of the New India*, p. 11.

[2] No definite information is available as to the origin of this name. Most probably it was given by Mathur Babu, as Ramlal., Sri Rama-krishna's nephew, has said, quoting the authority of his uncle himself.

Sri Ramakrishna always held in the highest respect, gradually overcame his disapproval, and he began to feel at home.

Within a very short time Sri Ramakrishna attracted the notice of Mathur Babu, who was impressed by the young man's religious fervour and wanted him to participate in the worship in the Kāli temple. But Sri Ramakrishna loved his freedom and was indifferent to any worldly career. The profession of the priesthood in a temple founded by a rich woman did not appeal to his mind. Further, he hesitated to take upon himself the responsibility for the ornaments and jewelry of the temple. Mathur had to wait for a suitable occasion.

At this time there came to Dakshineswar a youth of sixteen, destined to play an important role in Sri Ramakrishna's life. Hriday, a distant nephew[3] of Sri Ramakrishna, hailed from Sihore, a village not far from Kāmārpukur, and had been his boyhood friend. Clever, exceptionally energetic, and endowed with great presence of mind, he moved, as will be seen later, like a shadow about his uncle and was always ready to help him even at the sacrifice of his personal comfort. He was destined to be a mute witness of many of the spiritual experiences of Sri Ramakrishna and the caretaker of his body during the stormy days of his spiritual practice. Hriday came to Dakshineswar in search of a job, and Sri Ramakrishna was glad to see him.

Unable to resist the persuasion of Mathur Babu, Sri Ramakrishna at last entered the temple service, on condition that Hriday should be asked to assist him. His first duty was to dress and decorate the image of Kāli.

---

3 Hriday's mother was the daughter of Sri Ramakrishna's aunt (Khudiram's sister). Such a degree of relationship is termed in Bengal that of a " distant nephew."

One day the priest of the Rādhākānta temple accidentally dropped the image of Krishna on the floor, breaking one of its legs. The pundits advised the Rānī to install a new image, since the worship of an image with a broken limb was against the scriptural injunctions. But the Rānī was fond of the image, and she asked Sri Ramakrishna's opinion. In an abstracted mood, he said: " This solution is ridiculous. If a son-in-law of the Rānī broke his leg, would she discard him and put another in his place? Wouldn't she rather arrange for his treatment? Why should she not do the same thing in this case too? Let the image be repaired and worshipped as before." It was a simple, straightforward solution and was accepted by the Rānī. Sri Ramakrishna himself mended the break. The priest was dismissed for his carelessness, and at Mathur Babu's earnest request Sri Ramakrishna accepted the office of priest in the Rādhākānta temple.

SRI RAMAKRISHNA AS A PRIEST

Born in an orthodox brāhmin family Sri Ramakrishna knew the formalities of worship, its rites and rituals. The innumerable gods and goddesses of the Hindu religion are the human aspects of the indescribable and incomprehensible Spirit, as conceived by the finite human mind. They understand and appreciate human love and emotion, help men to realize their secular and spiritual ideals, and ultimately enable men to attain liberation from the miseries of phenomenal life. The source of light, intelligence, wisdom, and strength is the One alone from whom comes the fulfilment of desire. Yet as long as a man is bound by his human limitations, he cannot but worship God through human forms. He must use human symbols. Therefore Hinduism asks the devotees to look on God as the ideal father, the ideal mother, the ideal husband, the ideal son, or the ideal friend. But the name ultimately leads to the Nameless, the form to the formless, the

word to the silence, the emotion to the serene realization
of peace in Existence-Knowledge-Bliss Absolute. The gods
gradually merge in the one God. But until that realization is
achieved, the devotee cannot dissociate human factors from his
worship. Therefore the Deity is bathed and clothed and decked
with ornaments. He is fed and put to sleep. He is propitiated
with hymns, songs and prayers. And there are appropriate rites
connected with all these functions. For instance, to secure for
himself external purity, the priest bathes himself in holy water
and puts on a holy cloth. He purifies the mind and the
sense-organs by appropriate meditations. He fortifies the place of
worship against evil forces by drawing around it circles of fire
and water. He awakens the different spiritual centres of the
body and invokes the supreme Spirit in his heart. Then he
transfers the supreme Spirit to the image before him and
worships the image, regarding it no longer as clay or stone,
but as the embodiment of spirit, throbbing with life and
consciousness. After the worship the supreme Spirit is recalled
from the image to its true sanctuary, the heart of the priest.
The real devotee knows the absurdity of worshipping the
transcendental Reality with material articles—clothing That
which pervades the whole universe and the beyond, putting on a
pedestal That which cannot be limited by space, feeding That
which is disembodied and incorporeal, singing before That whose
glory the music of the spheres tries vainly to proclaim. But
through these rites the devotee aspires to go ultimately beyond
rites and rituals, forms and names, words and praise, and to
realize God as the all-pervading consciousness.

Hindu priests are thoroughly acquainted with the rites of
worship, but few of them are aware of their underlying significance. They move their hands and limbs mechanically, in
obedience to the letter of the scriptures, and repeat the holy man-

tras like parrots. But from the very beginning the inner meaning
of these rites was revealed to Sri Ramakrishna. As he sat facing
the image, a strange transformation came over his mind. While
going through the prescribed ceremonies, he would actually find
himself encircled by a wall of fire protecting him and the place of
worship from unspiritual vibrations, or he would feel the rising of
the mystic Kundalini through the different centres of the body.
The glow on his face, his deep absorption, and the intense
atmosphere of the temple impressed everyone who saw him
worship the Deity.

Ramkumar wanted Sri Ramakrishna to learn the intricate
rituals of the worship of Kāli. To become a priest of Kāli one
must undergo a special form of initiation from a qualified guru,
and for Sri Ramakrishna a suitable brāhmin was found. But no
sooner did the brāhmin speak the holy word in his ear than
Sri Ramakrishna, overwhelmed with emotion, uttered a loud cry
and plunged into deep concentration.

Mathur begged Sri Ramakrishna to take charge of the
worship in the Kāli temple. The young priest pleaded his
incompetence and his ignorance of the scriptures. Mathur
insisted that devotion and sincerity would more than compensate
for any lack of formal knowledge and make the divine Mother
manifest Herself through the image. In the end Sri Ramakrishna
had to yield to Mathur's request. He became the priest
of Kāli.

In 1856 Ramkumar breathed his last. Sri Ramakrishna
had already witnessed more than one death in the family. He
had come to realize how impermanent is life on earth. The
more he was convinced of the transitory nature of worldly things,
the more eager he became to realize God, the fountain of
immortality.

THE FIRST VISION OF KĀLI

And, indeed, he soon discovered what a strange Goddess he had chosen to serve. He became gradually enmeshed in the web of Her all-pervading presence. To the ignorant She is, to be sure, the image of destruction; but he found in Her the benign, all-loving Mother. Her neck is encircled with a garland of heads, and Her waist with a girdle of human arms, and two of Her hands hold weapons of death, and Her eyes dart a glance of fire; but, strangely enough, Ramakrishna felt in Her breath the soothing touch of tender love and saw in Her the seed of immortality. She stands on the bosom of Her consort, Siva; it is because She is the S'akti, the Power, inseparable from the Absolute. She is surrounded by jackals and other unholy creatures, the denizens of the cremation-ground. But is not the ultimate reality above holiness and unholiness? She appears to be reeling under the spell of wine. But who would create this mad world unless under the influence of a divine drunkenness? She is the highest symbol of all the forces of nature, the synthesis of their antinomies, the ultimate divine in the form of woman. She now became to Sri Ramakrishna the only reality, and the world became an unsubstantial shadow. Into Her worship he poured his soul. Before him She stood as the transparent portal to the shrine of ineffable reality.

The worship in the temple intensified Sri Ramakrishna's yearning for a living vision of the Mother of the universe. He began to spend in meditation the time not actually employed in the temple service; and for this purpose he selected an extremely solitary place. A deep jungle, thick with underbrush and prickly plants, lay to the north of the temples. Used at one time as a burial-ground, it was shunned by people even during the day-time for fear of ghosts. There Sri Ramakrishna began to spend the whole night in meditation, returning to his room only in the morning with eyes swollen as though from much weeping. While meditating, he would lay aside his cloth and his brāhminical thread. Explaining this strange conduct, he once said to Hriday: " Don't you know that when one thinks of God one should be freed from all ties ? From our very birth we have the eight fetters of hatred, shame, lineage, pride of good conduct, fear, secretiveness, caste, and grief. The sacred thread reminds me that I am a brāhmin and therefore superior to all. When calling on the Mother, one has to set aside all such ideas." Hriday thought his uncle was becoming insane.

As his love for God deepened, he began either to forget or to drop the formalities of worship. Sitting before the image, he would spend hours singing the devotional songs of great devotees of the Mother, such as Kamalākānta and Rāmprasād. Those rhapsodical songs, describing the direct vision of God, only intensified Sri Ramakrishna's longing. He felt the pangs of a child separated from its mother. Sometimes, in agony, he would rub his face against the ground and weep so bitterly that people, thinking he had lost his earthly mother, would sympathize with him in his grief. Sometimes, in moments of scepticism, he would cry: " Art Thou true, Mother, or is it all fiction—mere poetry without any reality ? If Thou dost exist, why do I not see Thee ? Is religion a mere fantasy and art Thou only a figment of man's imagination ? " Sometimes he would sit on the prayer carpet for two hours like an inert object. He began to behave in an abnormal manner, most of the time unconscious of the world. He almost gave up food; and sleep left him altogether.

But he did not have to wait very long. He has thus described his first vision of the Mother: " I felt as if my heart were being squeezed like a wet towel. I was overpowered with a great restlessness and a fear that it might not be my lot to realize Her in this life. I could not bear the separation from

Her any longer. Life seemed to be not worth living. Suddenly my glance fell on the sword that was kept in the Mother's temple. I determined to put an end to my life. When I jumped up like a madman and seized it, suddenly the blessed Mother revealed Herself. The buildings with their different parts, the temple, and everything else vanished from my sight, leaving no trace whatsoever, and in their stead I saw a limitless, infinite, effulgent ocean of consciousness. As far as the eye could see, the shining billows were madly rushing at me from all sides with a terrific noise, to swallow me up! I was panting for breath. I was caught in the rush and collapsed, unconscious. What was happening in the outside world I did not know; but within me there was a steady flow of undiluted bliss, altogether new, and I felt the presence of the divine Mother." On his lips, when he regained consciousness of the world was the word " Mother."

CHAPTER III

GOD-INTOXICATED STATE

YET this was only a foretaste of the intense experiences to come. The first glimpse of the divine Mother made him the more eager for Her uninterrupted vision. He wanted to see Her both in meditation and with eyes open. But the Mother began to play a teasing game of hide-and-seek with him, intensifying both his joy and his suffering. Weeping bitterly during the moments of separation from Her, he would pass into a trance and then find Her standing before him, smiling, talking, consoling, bidding him be of good cheer, and instructing him. During this period of spiritual practice he had many uncommon experiences. When he sat to meditate, he would hear strange clicking sounds in the joints of his legs, as if someone were locking them up, one after the other, to keep him motionless; and at the conclusion of his meditation he would again hear the same sounds, this time unlocking them and leaving him free to move about. He would see flashes like a swarm of fire-flies floating before his eyes, or a sea of deep mist around him, with luminous waves of molten silver. Again, in a sea of translucent mist he would behold the Mother first Her feet, then Her waist, body, face, and head, finally Her whole person; he would feel Her breath and hear Her voice. Worshipping in the temple, sometimes he would become exalted, sometimes he would remain motionless as stone, sometimes he would almost collapse from excessive emotion. Many of his actions, contrary to all tradition, seemed sacrilegious to the people. He would take a flower and touch it to his own head, body, and feet, and then offer it to the Goddess. Or, like a drunkard, he would reel to the throne of the Mother, touch Her chin by way of showing his affection for Her, and sing, talk, joke, laugh, and dance. Or he would take a morsel of food from the plate and hold it to Her mouth, begging Her to eat it, and would not be satisfied till he was convinced that She had really eaten. After the Mother had been put to sleep at night, from his own room he would hear Her ascending to the upper storey of the temple with the light steps of a happy girl, Her anklets jingling. Then he would discover Her standing with flowing hair, Her black form silhouetted against the sky of the night, looking at the Ganges or at the distant lights of Calcutta.

Naturally the temple officials took him for an insane person. His worldly well-wishers brought him to skilled physicians; but no medicine could cure his malady. Many a time he doubted his sanity himself. For he had been sailing across an uncharted sea, with no earthly guide to direct him. His only haven of security was the divine Mother Herself. To Her he would pray: "I do not know what these things are. I am ignorant of mantras and the scriptures. Teach me, Mother, how to realize Thee' Who else can help me? Art Thou not my only refuge and guide?'. And the sustaining presence of the Mother never failed him in his distress or doubt. Even those who criticized his conduct were greatly impressed with his purity, guilelessness, truthfulness, integrity, and holiness. They felt an uplifting influence in his presence.

It is said that samadhi, or trance, no more than opens the portal of the spiritual realm. Sri Ramakrishna felt an unquenchable desire to enjoy God in various ways. For his meditation he built a place in the northern wooded section of the temple garden. With Hriday's help he planted there five sacred trees. The spot, known as the Panchavati, became the scene of many of his visions.

As his spiritual mood deepened, he more and more felt himself to be a child of the divine Mother, He learnt to surrender himself completely to Her will and let Her direct him.

" O Mother," he would constantly pray, " I have taken refuge in Thee. Teach me what to do and what to say. Thy will is paramount everywhere and is for the good of Thy children. Merge my will in Thy will and make me Thy instrument."

His visions became deeper and more intimate. He no longer had to meditate to behold the divine Mother. Even while retaining consciousness of the outer world, he would see Her as tangibly as the temples, the trees, the river, and the men around him.

On a certain occasion Mathur Babu stealthily entered the temple to watch the worship. He was profoundly moved by the young priest's devotion and sincerity. He realized that Sri Ramakrishna had transformed the stone image into the living Goddess.

Sri Ramakrishna one day fed a cat with the food that was to be offered to Kāli. This was too much for the manager of the temple-garden, who considered himself responsible for the proper conduct of the worship. He reported Sri Ramakrishna's insane behaviour to Mathur Babu.

Sri Ramakrishna has described the incident: " The divine Mother revealed to me in the Kāli temple that it was She who had become everything. She showed me that everything was full of consciousness. The image was consciousness, the altar was consciousness, the water-vessels were consciousness, the door-sill was consciousness, the marble floor was consciousness— all was consciousness. I found everything inside the room soaked, as it were, in bliss—the bliss of God. I saw a wicked man in front of the Kāli temple; but in him also I saw the power of the divine Mother vibrating. That was why I fed a cat with the food that was to be offered to the divine Mother. I clearly perceived that all this was the divine Mother—even the cat.

The manager of the temple garden wrote to Mathur Bābu saying that I was feeding the cat with the offering intended for the divine Mother. But Mathur Bābu had insight into the state of my mind. He wrote back to the manager : ' Let him do whatever he likes. You must not say anything to him.'"

One of the painful ailments from which Sri Ramakrishna suffered at this time was a burning sensation in his body, and he was cured by a strange vision. During worship in the temple, following the scriptural injunctions, he would imagine the presence of the " sinner " in himself and the destruction of this " sinner." One day he was meditating in the Panchavati, when he saw come out of him a red-eyed man of black complexion, reeling like a drunkard. Soon there emerged from him another person, of serene countenance, wearing the ochre cloth of a sannyāsi and carrying in his hand a trident. The second person attacked the first and killed him with the trident. Thereafter Sri Ramakrishna was free of his pain.

About this time he began to worship God by assuming the attitude of a servant toward his master. He imitated the mood of Hanumān, the monkey-chieftain of the *Ramayana*, the ideal servant of Rama and traditional model for this self-effacing form of devotion. When he meditated on Hanumān his movements and his way of life began to resemble those of a monkey. His eyes became restless. He lived on fruits and roots. With his cloth tied around his waist, a portion of it hanging in the form of a tail, he jumped from place to place instead of walking. And after a short while he was blessed with a vision of Sīta, the divine consort of Rama, who entered his body and disappeared there with the words, ". I bequeath to you my smile."

Mathur had faith in the sincerity of Sri Ramakrishna's spiritual zeal, but began now to doubt his sanity. He had watched him jumping about like a monkey. One day, when Rāni

Rāsmani was listening to Sri Ramakrishna's singing in the temple, the young priest abruptly turned and slapped her. Apparently listening to his song, she had actually been thinking of a law-suit. She accepted the punishment as though the divine Mother Herself had imposed it : but Mathur was distressed. He begged Sri Ramakrishna to keep his feelings under control and to heed the conventions of society. God Himself, he argued, follows laws. God never permitted, for instance, flowers of two colours to grow on the same stalk. The following day Sri Ramakrishna presented Mathur Bābu with two hibiscus flowers growing on the same stalk, one red and one white.

Mathur and Rānī Rāsmani began to ascribe the mental ailment of Sri Ramakrishna in part, at least, to his observance of rigid continence. Thinking that a natural life would relax the tension of his nerves, they engineered a plan with two women of ill fame. But as soon as the women entered his room, Sri Ramakrishna beheld in them the manifestation of the divine Mother of the universe and went into samadhi uttering Her name.

HALADHĀRĪ

In 1858 there came to Dakshineswar a cousin of Sri Rama-krishna, Haladhārī by name, who was to remain there about eight years. On account of Sri Ramakrishna's indifferent health, Mathur appointed this man to the office of priest in the Kāli temple. He was a complex character, versed in the letter of the scriptures, but hardly aware of their spirit. He loved to participate in hair-splitting theological discussions and, by the measure of his own erudition, he proceeded to gauge Sri Rama-krishna. An orthodox brāhmin, he thoroughly disapproved of his cousin's unorthodox actions, but he was not unimpressed by Sri Ramakrishna's purity of life, ecstatic love of God, and yearning for realization.

R—3

One day Haladhāri upset Sri Ramakrishna with the statement that God is incomprehensible to the human mind. Sri Rāmakrishna has described the great moment of doubt when he wondered whether his visions had really misled him: " With sobs I prayed to the Mother, ' Canst Thou have the heart to deceive me like this because I am a fool ?' A stream of tears flowed from my eyes. Shortly afterwards I saw a volume of mist rising from the floor and filling the space before me. In the midst of it there appeared a face with flowing beard, calm, highly expressive, and fair. Fixing its gaze steadily upon me, it said solemnly, ' Remain in bhāvamukha on the threshold of relative consciousness.' This it repeated three times and then it gently disappeared in the mist, which itself dissolved. This vision reassured me."

A garbled report of Sri Ramakrishna's failing health, indifference to worldly life, and various abnormal activities reached Kāmārpukur and filled the heart of his poor mother with anguish. At her repeated request he returned to his village for a change of air. But his boyhood friends did not interest him any more. A divine fever was consuming him. He spent a great part of the day and night in one of the cremation grounds, in meditation. The place reminded him of the impermanence of the human body, of human hopes and achievements. It also reminded him of Kāli, the Goddess of destruction.

MARRIAGE AND AFTER

But in a few months his health showed improvement, and he recovered to some extent his natural buoyancy of spirit. His happy mother was encouraged to think it might be a good time to arrange his marriage. The boy was now twenty-three years old. A wife would bring him back to earth. And she was delighted when her son welcomed her suggestion. Perhaps he saw in it the finger of God.

Sāradāmani, a little girl of five, lived in the neighbouring village of Jayrāmbāti. Even at this age she had been praying to God to make her character as stainless and fragrant as the white tuberose. Looking at the full moon, she would say: "O God, there are dark spots even on the moon. But make my character spotless." It was she who was selected as the bride for Sri Ramakrishna.

The marriage ceremony was duly performed. Such early marriage in India is in the nature of a betrothal, the marriage being consummated when the girl attains puberty. But in this case the marriage remained for ever unconsummated. Sri Ramakrishna lived at Kāmārpukur about a year and a half and then returned to Dakshineswar.

Hardly had he crossed the threshold of the Kāli temple when he found himself again in the whirlwind. His madness reappeared tenfold. The same meditation and prayer, the same ecstatic moods, the same burning sensation, the same weeping, the same sleeplessness, the same indifference to the body and the outside world, the same divine delirium. He subjected himself to fresh disciplines in order to eradicate greed and lust, the two great impediments to spiritual progress. With a rupee in one hand and some earth in the other, he would reflect on the comparative value of these two for the realization of God, and finding them equally worthless he would toss them, with equal indifference, into the Ganges. Women he regarded as the manifestations of the divine Mother. Never even in a dream did he feel the impulses of lust. And to root out of his mind the idea of caste superiority, he cleaned a pariah's house with his long and neglected hair. When he would sit in meditation, birds would perch on his head and peck in his hair for grains of food. Snakes would crawl over his body, and neither would be aware of the other. Sleep left him altogether. Day and night, visions flitted before him. He saw the sannyāsi who had previously killed the "sinner" in him again coming out of his body, threatening him with the trident, and ordering him to concentrate on God. Or the same sannyāsi would visit distant places, following a luminous path, and bring him reports of what was happening there. Sri Ramakrishna used to say later that in the case of an advanced devotee the mind itself becomes the guru, living and moving like an embodied being.

Rāni Rāsmani, the foundress of the temple-garden, passed away in 1861. After her death, her son-in-law Mathur became the sole executor of the estate. He placed himself and his resources at the disposal of Sri Ramakrishna and began to look after his physical comfort. Sri Ramakrishna later spoke of him as one of his five "suppliers of stores" appointed by the divine Mother. Whenever a desire arose in his mind, Mathur fulfilled it without hesitation.

THE BRĀHMANĪ

There came to Dakshineswar at this time a brāhmin woman who was to play an important part in Sri Ramakrishna's spiritual unfoldment. Born in East Bengal, she was an adept in the Tāntrik and Vaishnava methods of worship. She was slightly over fifty years of age, handsome, and garbed in the orange robe of a nun. Her sole possessions were a few books and two pieces of wearing-cloth.

Sri Ramakrishna welcomed the visitor with great respect, described to her his experiences and visions, and told her of people's belief that these were symptoms of madness. She listened to him attentively and said : " My son, everyone in this world is mad. Some are mad for money, some for creature comforts, some for name and fame; and you are mad for God." She assured him that he was passing through the almost unknown spiritual experience described in the scriptures as mahābhāva, the most exalted rapture of divine love. She told him that this extreme exaltation had been described as manifesting itself through nineteen physical symptoms including the shedding of tears, a tremor of the body, horripilation, perspiration, and a burning sensation. The bhakti scriptures, she declared, had recorded only two instances of the experience, namely those of Sri Rādhā and Sri Chaitanya.

Very soon a tender relationship sprang up between Sri Ramakrishna and the Brāhmanī, she looking upon him as the baby Krishna, and he upon her as mother. Day after day she watched his ecstasy during the kirtan and meditation, his samādhi, his mad yearning; and she recognized in him a power to transmit spirituality to others. She came to the conclusion that such things were not possible for an ordinary devotee, not even for a highly developed soul. Only an Incarnation of God was capable of such spiritual manifestations. She proclaimed openly that Sri Ramakrishna, like Sri Chaitanya, was an Incarnation of God.

When Sri Ramakrishna told Mathur what the Brāhmanī had said about him, Mathur shook his head in doubt. He was reluctant to accept him as an Incarnation of God, an Avatāra comparable to Rama, Krishna, Buddha, and Chaitanya, though he admitted Sri Ramakrishna's extraordinary spirituality. Whereupon the Brāhmanī asked Mathur to arrange a conference of scholars who should discuss the matter with her. He agreed to the proposal and the meeting was arranged. It was to be held in the nāt-mandir in front of the Kāli temple.

Two famous pundits of the time were invited: Vaishnava-charan, the leader of the Vaishnava society, and Gauri. The first to arrive was Vaishnavacharan, with a distinguished company of scholars and devotees. The Brāhmanī, like a proud mother, proclaimed her view before him and supported it with quotations from the scriptures. As the pundits discussed the deep theological question, Sri Ramakrishna, perfectly indifferent to everything happening around him, sat in their midst like a child, immersed in his own thoughts, sometimes smiling, sometimes chewing a pinch of spices from a pouch, or again saying to Vaishnavacharan with a nudge: "Look here, sometimes I feel like this, too." Presently, Vaishnavacharan arose to declare himself in total agreement with the view of the Brāhmanī. He declared that Sri Ramakrishna had undoubtedly experienced mahābhāva and that this was the certain sign of the rare manifestation of God in a man. The people assembled there, especially the officers of the temple garden were struck dumb. Sri Ramakrishna said to Mathur, like a boy: "Just fancy, he too says so! Well, I am glad to learn that after all it is not a disease."

When, a few days later, pundit Gauri arrived, another meeting was held, and he agreed with the view of the Brāhmanī and Vaishnavacharan. To Sri Ramakrishna's remark that Vaishnavcharan had declared him to be an Avatāra, Gauri replied: "Is that all he has to say about you? Then he has said very little. I am fully convinced that you are that mine of spiritual power, only a small fraction of which descends on earth, from time to time, in the form of an Incarnation."

"Ah!" said Sri Ramakrishna with a smile, "you seem to have quite outbid Vaishnavacharan in this matter. What have you found in me that makes you entertain such an idea?"

Gauri said: "I feel it in my heart and I have the scriptures on my side. I am ready to prove it to anyone who challenges me."

"Well," Sri Ramakrishna said, "it is you who say so, but believe me, I know nothing about it."

Thus the insane priest was by verdict of the great scholars of the day proclaimed a divine Incarnation. His visions were not the result of an over-heated brain; they had precedent in spiritual history. And how did the proclamation affect Sri Ramakrishna himself? He remained the simple child of the Mother that he had been since the first day of his life. Years later, when two of his householder disciples openly spoke of him as a divine Incarnation and the matter was reported to him, he said with a touch of sarcasm: "Do they think they will enhance my glory that way? One of them is an actor on the stage and the other a physician. What do they know about Incarnations? Why, years ago pundits like Gauri and Vaishnavacharan declared me to be an Avatāra. They were great scholars and knew what they said. But that did not make any change in my mind."

Sri Ramakrishna was a learner all his life. He often used to quote a proverb to his disciples: "Friend, the more I live the more I learn." When the excitement created by the Brāhmani's declaration was over, he set himself to the task of practising spiritual disciplines according to the traditional methods laid down in the Tantra and Vaishnava scriptures. Hitherto he had pursued his spiritual ideal according to the promptings of his own mind and heart. Now he accepted the Brāhmani as his guru and set foot on the traditional highways.

TANTRA

According to the Tantra, the ultimate reality is Chit, or Consciousness, which is identical with Sat, or Being, and with Ānanda, or Bliss. This ultimate reality, Satchidānanda, Existence-Knowledge-Bliss Absolute, is identical with the reality preached in the Vedas. And man is identical with this reality; but under the influence of māyā, or illusion, he has forgotten his true nature. He takes to be real a merely apparent world of subject and object, and this error is the cause of his bondage and suffering.   The goal of spiritual discipline is the rediscovery of his true identity with the divine Reality.

For the achievement of this goal the Vedanta prescribes an austere negative method of discrimination and renunciation, which can be followed by only a few individuals endowed with sharp intelligence and unshakable will-power.   But Tantra takes into consideration the natural weakness of human beings, their lower appetites, and their love for the concrete.   It combines philosophy with rituals, meditation with ceremonies, renunciation with enjoyment.   The underlying purpose is gradually to train the aspirant to meditate on his identity with the Ultimate.

The average man wishes to enjoy the material objects of the world. Tantra bids him enjoy these, but at the same time discovers in them the presence of God.   Mystical rites are prescribed by which, slowly, the sense objects become spiritualized and sense attraction is transformed into love of God.   So the very "bonds" of man are turned into "releasers".   The very poison that kills is transmuted into the elixir of life.   Outward renunciation is not necessary.   Thus the aim of Tantra is to sublimate bhoga or enjoyment, into yoga or union with Consciousness. For, according to this philosophy, the world with all its manifestations is nothing but the sport of Śiva and Śakti, the absolute and its inscrutable power.

The disciplines of Tantra are graded to suit aspirants of all degrees.   Exercises are prescribed for people with "animal" "heroic," and "divine" outlooks.   Certain of the rites require the presence of members of the opposite sex.   Here the aspirant learns to look on woman as the embodiment of the goddess Kāli, the Mother of the universe.   The very basis of Tantra is the Motherhood of God and the glorification of woman.   Every part of a woman's body is to be regarded as incarnate Divinity. But the rights are extremely dangerous. The help of a qualified guru is absolutely necessary. An unwary devotee may lose his foothold and fall into a pit of depravity.

According to the Tantra, Sakti is the active creation force in the universe. Siva, the Absolute, is a more or less passive principle. Further, Sakti is as inseparable from Siva as fire's power to burn is from fire itself. Sakti, the creative Power, contains in Its womb the universe, and therefore is the divine Mother. All women are Her symbols. Kāli is one of Her several forms. The meditation on Kāli, creative Power, is the central discipline of the Tantra. While meditating, the aspirant at first regards himself as one with the Absolute and then thinks that out of that impersonal Consciousness emerge two entities, namely, his own self and the living form of the Goddess. He then projects the Goddess into the tangible image before him and worships it as the divine Mother.

Sri Ramakrishna set himself to the task of practising the disciplines of Tantra; and at the bidding of the divine Mother Herself, he accepted the Brāhmani as his guru. He performed profound and delicate ceremonies in the Panchavati and under the bel-tree at the northern extremity of the temple compound. He practised all the disciplines of the sixty-four principal Tantra books, and it took him never more than three days to achieve the result promised in any one of them. After the observance of a few preliminary rites, he would be overwhelmed with a strange divine fervour and would go into samadhi, where his mind would dwell in exaltation. Evil ceased to exist for him. The word "carnal" lost its meaning. The whole world and everything in it appeared as the lilā, the sport, of Siva and Sakti He beheld everywhere manifest the power and beauty of the Mother; the whole world, animate and inanimate, appeared to him as pervaded with Chit, Consciousness, and with Ānanda, Bliss.

He saw in a vision the ultimate Cause of the universe as a huge luminous triangle giving birth every moment to an infinite number of worlds. He heard the Anāhata S'abda, the great sound Om, of which the innumerable sounds of the universe are only so many echoes. He acquired the eight supernatural powers of yoga, which make a man almost omnipotent, and these he spurned as of no value whatsoever to the spirit. He had a vision of the divine māyā, the inscrutable power of God, by which the universe is created and sustained, and into which it is finally absorbed. In this vision he saw a woman of exquisite beauty, about to become a mother, emerging from the Ganges and slowly approaching the Panchavati. Presently she gave birth to a child and began to nurse it tenderly. A moment later she assumed a terrible aspect, seized the child with her grim jaws, and crushed it. Swallowing it, she re-entered the waters of the Ganges.

But the most remarkable experience during this period was the awakening of the Kundalini Sakti, the "Serpent Power". He actually saw the power, at first lying asleep at the bottom of the spinal column, then waking up and ascending along the mystic Sushumnā canal and through its six centres, or lotuses, to the Sahasrarā, the thousand-petalled lotus in the top of the head. He further saw that as the Kundalini went upward the different lotuses bloomed. And this phenomenon was accompanied by visions and trances. Later on he described to his disciples and devotees the various movements of the Kundalini : the fish-like, bird-like, monkey-like, and so on. The awakening of the Kundalini is the beginning of spiritual consciousness, and its union with S'iva in the Sahasrāra, ending in samādhi, is the consummation of the Tāntrik disciplines.

About this time it was revealed to him that in a short while many devotees would seek his guidance.

VAISHNAVA DISCIPLINES

After completing the Tāntrik sādhanā Sri Ramakrishna followed the Brāhmani in the disciplines of Vaishnavism. The Vaisihnavas are ·worshippers of Vishnu, the " All-pervading ", the supreme God, who is also known as Hari and Nārāyana. Of Vishnu's various Incarnations the two with the largest number of followers are Rama and Krishna.

Vaishnavism is exclusively a religion of bhakti. Bhakti is intense love of God, attachment to Him alone; it is of the nature of bliss and bestows upon the lover immortality and liberation. God, according to Vaishnavism, cannot be realized through logic or reason; and, without bhakti, all penances, austerities, and rites are futile. Man cannot realize God by self-exertion alone. For the vision of God His grace is absolutely necessary, and this grace is felt by the pure of heart. The mind is to be purified through bhakti. The pure mind then remains for ever immersed in the ecstasy of God-vision. It is the cultivation of this divine love that is the chief concern of the Vaishnava religion.

There are three kinds of formal devotion: tāmasic, rājasic, and sāttvic. If a person, while showing devotion to God, is actuated by malevolence, arrogance, jealousy or anger, then his devotion is tāmasic, since it is influenced by tamas, the quality of inertia. If he worships God from a desire for fame or wealth, or from any other worldly ambition, then his devotion is rājasic, since it is influenced by rajas, the quality of activity. But if a person loves God without any thought of material gain, if he performs his duties to please God alone and maintains toward all created beings the attitude of friendship, then his devotion is called sāttvic, since it is influenced by sattva, the quality of harmony. But the highest devotion transcends the three gunas or qualities, being a spontaneous, uninterrupted inclination of the mind toward God, the inner Soul of all beings; and it wells up in the heart of a true devotee as soon as he hears the name of God or mention of God's attributes. A devotee possessed of this love would not accept the happiness of heaven if it were offered him. His one desire is to love God under all conditions—in pleasure and pain, life and death, honour and dishonour, prosperity and adversity.

There are two stages of bhakti. The first is known as vaidhī-bhakti, or love of God qualified by scriptural injunctions. For the devotees of this stage are prescribed regular and methodical worship, hymns, prayers, the repetition of God's name, and the chanting of His glories. This lower bhakti in course of time matures into parā-bhakti, or supreme devotion, known also as prema, the most intense form of divine love. Divine love is an end in itself. It exists potentially in all human hearts, but in the case of bound creatures it is misdirected to earthly objects.

To develop the devotee's love for God, Vaishnavism humanizes God. God is to be regarded as the devotee's parent, master, friend, child, husband, or sweetheart, each succeeding relationship representing an intensification of love. These bhāvas, or attitudes toward God are known as śānta, dāsya, sakhya, vātsalya, and madhura. The rishis of the Vedas, Hanumān, the cowherd boys of Vrindavan, Rama's mother Kausalyā, and Rādhikā, Krishna's sweetheart, exhibited, respectively, the most perfect examples of these forms. In the ascending scale the glories of God are gradually forgotten and the devotee realizes more and more the intimacy of divine communion. Finally he regards himself as the mistress of his Beloved, and no artificial barrier remains to separate him from his Ideal. No social or moral obligation can bind to the earth his soaring spirit. He experiences perfect union

with the Godhead. Unlike the Vedantist, who strives to tran-
scend all varieties of the subject-object relationship, a devotee of
the Vaishnava path wishes to retain both his own individuality
and the personality of God. To him God is not an intangible
Absolute, but the Purushottama, the supreme Person.

While practising the discipline of the madhura bhāva, the
male devotee often regards himself as a woman, in order to develop the most intense form of love for Sri Krishna, the only
purusha, or man, in the universe. This assumption of the attitude
of the opposite sex has a deep psychological significance. It is a
matter of common experience that an idea may be cultivated to
such an intense degree that every idea alien to it is driven from
the mind. This peculiarity of the mind may be utilized for the
subjugation of the lower desires and the development of the
spiritual nature. Now, the idea which is the basis of all desires
and passions in a man is the conviction of his indissoluble association with a male body. If he can inoculate himself thoroughly
with the idea that he is a woman, he can get rid of the desires
peculiar to his male body. Again, the idea that he is a woman
may in turn be made to give way to another higher idea, namely,
that he is neither man nor woman, but the impersonal Spirit.
alone can enjoy real communion with the impersonal God.
Hence the highest realization of the Vaishnava draws close to the
transcendental experience of the Vedantist.

A beautiful expression of the Vaishnava worship of God
through love is to be found in the Vrindāvan episode of the
Bhagavata. The gopis, or milk-maids of Vrindāvan regarded the
six-year-old Krishna as their Beloved. They sought no personal
gain or happiness from this love. They surrendered to Krishna
their bodies, minds, and souls. Of all the gopis, Rādhikā, or
Rādhā, because of her intense love for Him, was the closest to
Krishna. She manifested mahābhāva and was united with her

Beloved. This union represents through sensuous language, a supersensuous experience.

Sri Chaitanya, also known as Gaurānga, Gorā, or Nimāi, born in Bengal in 1485 and regarded as an Incarnation of God, is a great prophet of the Vaishnava religion. Chaitanya declared the chanting of God's name to be the most efficacious spiritual discipline for the Kaliyuga.

Sri Ramakrishna, as the monkey Hanumān, had already. worshipped God as his Master. Through his devotion to Kāli he had worshipped God as his Mother. He was now to take up the other relationships prescribed by the Vaishnava scriptures.

RĀMLĀLĀ

About the year 1864 there came to Dakshineswar a wandering Vaishnava monk, Jatādhārī, whose ideal deity was Rama He always carried with him a small metal image of the deity, which he called by the endearing name of Rāmlālā, the boy Rama. Toward this little image he displayed the tender affection of Kausalyā for her divine son, Rama. As a result of lifelong spiritual practice he had actually found in the metal image the presence of his Ideal. Rāmlālā was no longer for him a metal image, but the living God. He devoted himself to nursing Rama, feeding Rama, playing with Rama, taking Rama for a walk, and bathing Rama. And he found that the image responded to his love.

Sri Ramakrishna, much impressed with his devotion, requested Jatādhārī to spend a few days at Dakshineswar. Soon Rāmlālā became the favourite companion of Sri Ramakrishna too. Later on he described to the devotees how the little image would dance gracefully before him, jump on his back, insist on being taken in his arms, run to the fields in the sun, pluck flowers from the bushes, and play pranks like a naughty boy. A very sweet relationship sprang up between him and Rāmlālā, for whom he felt the love of a mother.

One day Jatādharī requested Sri Ramakrishna to keep the image and bade him adieu with tearful eyes. He declared that Rāmlālā had fulfilled his innermost prayer and that he now had no more need of formal worship. A few days later Sri Ramakrishna was blessed through Rāmlālā with a vision of Ramachandra, whereby he realized that the Rama of the *Ramayana*, the son of Dasaratha, pervades the whole universe as spirit and consciousness; that He is its Creator, Sustainer, and Destroyer; that, in still another aspect, He is the transcendental Brahman, without form, attribute, or name.

While worshipping Rāmlālā as the divine child, Sri Ramakrishna's heart became filled with motherly tenderness, and he began to regard himself as a woman. His speech and gestures changed. He began to move freely with the ladies of Mathur's family, who now looked upon him as one of their own sex. During this time he worshipped the divine Mother as Her companion or handmaid.

IN COMMUNION WITH THE DIVINE BELOVED

Sri Ramakrishna now devoted himself to scaling the most inaccessible and dizzy heights of dualistic worship, namely, the complete union with Sri Krishna as the beloved of the heart. He regarded himself as one of the gopis of Vrindāvan, mad with longing for her divine Sweetheart. At his request Mathur provided him with woman's dress and jewelry. In this love-pursuit, food and drink were forgotten. Day and night he wept bitterly. The yearning turned into a mad frenzy; for the divine Krishna began to play with him the old tricks He had played with the gopis. He would tease and taunt, now and then revealing Himself, but always keeping at a distance. Sri Ramakrishna's anguish brought on a return of the old physical symptoms: the burning sensation, an oozing of blood through the pores, a loosening of the joints, and the stopping of physiological functions.

The Vaishnava scriptures advise one to propitiate Rādhā and obtain her grace in order to realize Sri Krishna. So the tortured devotee now turned his prayer to her. Within a short time he enjoyed her blessed vision. He saw and felt the figure of Rādhā disappearing into his own body.

He said later on: " It is impossible to describe the heavenly beauty and sweetness of Rādhā, Her very appearance showed that she had completely forgotten herself in her passionate attachment to Krishna. Her complexion was light yellow."

Now one with Rādhā, he manifested the great ecstatic love, the mahābhāva, which had found in her its fullest expression. Later Sri Ramakrishna said: " The manifestation in the same individual of the nineteen different kinds of emotion for God is called, in the books on bhakti, mahābhāva. An ordinary man takes a whole lifetime to express even a single one of these. But in this body [meaning himself] there has been a complete manifestation of all nineteen."

The love of Rādhā is the precursor of the resplendent vision of Sri Krishna, and Sri Ramakrishna soon experienced that vision. The enchanting form of Krishna appeared to him and merged in his person. He became Krishna; he totally forgot his own individuality and the world; he saw Krishna in himself and in the universe. Thus he attained to the fulfilment of the worship of the personal God. He drank from the fountain of immortal Bliss. The agony of his heart vanished for ever. He realized Amrita, Immortality, beyond the shadow of death.

One day, listening to a recitation of the *Bhagavata* on the verandah of the Rādhākānta temple, he fell into a divine mood and saw the enchanting form of Krishna. He perceived the luminous rays issuing from Krishna's lotus feet in the form of a stout rope, which touched first the *Bhagavata* and then his own chest, connecting all three—God, the scripture, and the devotee. " After this vision", he used to say, " I came to realize that Bhagavān, Bhakta, and *Bhāgavata*—God, devotee, and scripture —are in reality one and the same."

VEDANTA

The Brāhmanī was the enthusiastic teacher and astonished beholder of Sri Ramakrishna in his spiritual progress. She became proud of the achievements of her unique pupil. But the pupil himself was not permitted to rest; his destiny beckoned him forward. His divine Mother would allow him no respite till he had left behind the entire realm of duality with its visions, experiences, and ecstatic dreams. But for the new ascent the old tender guides would not suffice. The Brāhmanī, on whom he had depended for three years, saw her son escape from her to follow the command of a teacher with masculine strength, a sterner mien, a gnarled physique, and a virile voice. The new guru was a wandering monk. The sturdy Totā Puri, whom Sri Ramakrishna learnt to address affectionately as Nāngtā, the " Naked One," because of his total renunciation of all earthly objects and attachments, including even a piece of wearing-cloth.

Totā Puri was the bearer of a philosophy new to Sri Rama krishna, the non-dualistic Vedanta philosophy, whose conclusions Totā Puri had experienced in his own life. This ancient Hindu system designates the ultimate Reality as Brahman, also described as Sātchidānanda, Existence-Knowledge-Bliss Absolute. Brahman is the only real Existence. In It there is no time, no space, no casuality, no multiplicity. But through māyā, Its inscrutable power, time, space, and causality are created and the One appears to break into the many. The eternal Spirit appears as a manifold of individuals endowed with form and subject to the conditions of time. The Immortal becomes a victim of birth and death. The Changeless undergoes change. The sinless pure Soul, hypnotized by Its own māyā, experiences the joys of heaven and the pains of hell. But these experiences based on the duality of the subject-object relationship are unreal. Even the vision of a personal God is, ultimately speaking, as illusory as the experience of any other object. Man attains his liberation, therefore, by piercing the veil of māyā and rediscovering his total identity with Brahman. Knowing himself to be one with the universal Spirit, he realizes ineffable peace. Only then does he go beyond the fiction of birth and death; only then does he become immortal. And this is the ultimate goal of all religions—to de-hypnotize the soul now hypnotized by its own ignorance.

The path of the Vedantic discipline in the path of negation, "Neti," in which, by stern determination, all that is unreal is both negated and renounced. It is the path of jnāna, knowledge, the direct method of realizing the Absolute. After the negation of everything relative, including the discriminating ego itself, the aspirant merges in the One without a second, in the bliss of nirvikalpa samādhi, where subject and object are alike dissolved. The soul goes beyond the realm of thought. The domain of duality is transcended. Māyā is left behind with all its changes and modifications. The real Man towers above the delusions of creation, preservation, and destruction. An avalanche of indescribable Bliss sweeps away all relative ideas of pain and pleasure, good and evil. There shines in the heart the glory of the eternal Brahman, Existence-Knowledge-Bliss Absolute. Knower, knowledge, and known are dissolved in the ocean of one eternal Consciousness ; love, lover, and beloved merge in the unbounded sea of supreme Felicity; birth, growth, and death vanish in infinite Existence. All doubts and misgivings are quelled for ever; the oscillations of the mind are stopped; the momentum of past actions is exhausted. Breaking down the ridge-pole of the tabernacle in which the soul has made its abode for untold ages, stilling the body, calming the mind, drowning the ego, the sweet joy of Brahman wells up in that superconscious state. Space disappears into nothingness, time is swallowed in eternity, and causation becomes a dream of the past. Only Existence is. Ah! Who can describe what the soul then feels in its communion with the Self?

Even when man descends from this dizzy height, he is devoid of ideas of " I " and " mine "; he looks on the body as a mere shadow, an outer sheath encasing the soul. He does not dwell on the past, takes no thought for the future, and looks with indifference on the present. He surveys everything in the world; with an eye of equality; he is no longer touched by the infinite variety of phenomena; he no longer reacts to pleasure and pain. He remains unmoved whether he—that is to say, his body—is worshipped by the good or tormented by the wicked; for he realizes that it is the one Brahman that manifests Itself through everything. The impact of such an experience devastates the body and mind. Consciousness becomes blasted, as it were, with an excess of Light. In the Vedanta books it is said that after the experience of nirvikalpa samadhi the body drops off like a dry leaf. Only those who are born with a special mission for the world can return from this height to the valleys of normal life. They live and move in the world for the welfare of mankind. They are invested with a supreme spiritual power. A divine glory shines through them.

TOTĀPURĪ

Totā Purī arrived at the Dakshineswar temple-garden toward the end of 1864. Perhaps born in the Punjab, he was the head of a monastery in that province of India and claimed leadership of seven hundred sannyāsis. Trained from early youth in the disciplines of the Advaita Vedanta, he looked upon the world as an illusion. The gods and goddesses of the dualistic worship were to him mere fantasies of the deluded mind. Prayers, ceremonies, rites, and rituals had nothing to do with true religion, and about these he was utterly indifferent. Exercising self-exertion and unshakable will-power, he had liberated himself from attachment to the sense-objects of the relative universe. For forty years he had practised austere discipline on the bank of the sacred Narmadā and had finally realized his identity with the Absolute. Thenceforward he roamed in the world as an unfettered soul, a lion free from the cage. Clad in a loin-cloth, he spent his days under the canopy of the sky alike in storm and sunshine, feeding his body on the slender pittance of alms. He had been visiting the estuary of the Ganges. On his return journey along the bank of the sacred river, led to the inscrutable divine will, he stopped at Dakshineswar.

Totā Purī, discovering at once that Sri Ramakrishna was prepared to be a student of Vedānta, agreed to initiate him into its mysteries. With the permission of the divine Mother, Sri Ramakrishna agreed to the proposal. But Totā Purī explained that only a sannyāsi could receive the teaching of Vedānta. Sri Ramakrishna agreed to renounce the world, but with the stipulation that the ceremony of his initiation into the monastic order be performed in secret, to spare the feelings of his old mother, who had been living with him at Dakshineswar.

On the appointed day, in the small hours of the morning, a fire was lighted in the Panchavatī. Totā Purī and Sri Ramakrishna sat before it. The flame played on their faces. "Ramakrishna was a small brown man with a short beard and beautiful eyes, long dark eyes, full of light, obliquely set and slightly veiled,

never very wide open, but seeing half-closed a great distance
both outwardly and inwardly. His mouth was open over his
white teeth in a bewitching smile, at once affectionate and
mischievous. Of medium height, he was thin to emaciation and
extremely delicate. His temperament was high-strung, for he
was supersensitive to all the winds of joy and sorrow, both moral
and physical. He was indeed a living reflection of all that
happened before the mirror of his eyes, a two-sided mirror, turned
both out and in."[4] Facing him, the other rose like a rock. He
was very tall and robust, a sturdy and tough oak. His constitu-
tion and mind were of iron. He was the strong leader of men.

In the burning flame before him Sri Ramakrishna performed
the rituals of destroying his attachment to relatives, friends,
body, mind, sense-organs, ego and the world. The leaping flame
swallowed it all, making the initiate free and pure. The sacred
thread and the tuft of hair were consigned to the fire, completing
his severance from caste, sex, and society. Last of all he burnt
in that fire, with all that is holy as his witness, his desire for
enjoyment here and hereafter. He uttered the sacred mantras
giving assurance of safety and fearlessness to all beings who
were only manifestations of his own Self. The rites completed,
the disciple received from the guru the loincloth and ochre robe,
the emblems of his new life.

The teacher and the disciple repaired to the meditation room
near by. Totā Purī began to impart to Sri Ramakrishna the great
truths of Vedanta.

"Brahman", he said, "is the only Reality, ever pure, ever
illumined, ever free, beyond the limits of time, space, and
causation. Though apparently divided by names and forms

---

[4] Romain Roliand, *Prophets of the New India,* pp. 38-9.

through the inscrutable power of māyā, that enchantress who makes the impossible possible, Brahman is really One and undivided. When a seeker merges in the beatitude of samādhi, he does not perceive time and space or name and form, the offspring of māyā. Whatever is within the domain of māyā is unreal. Give it up. Destroy the prison-house of name and form and rush out of it with the strength of a lion. Dive deep in search of the Self and realize It through samādhi. You will find the world of name and form vanishing into void, and the puny ego dissolving in Brahman-consciousness. You will realize your identity with Brahman, Existence-Knowledge-Bliss Absolute." Quoting the Upanishad, Totā Purī said: " That knowledge is shallow by which one sees or hears or knows another. What is shallow is worthless and can never give real felicity. But the knowledge by which one does not see another or hear another or know another, which is beyond duality, is great and through such knowledge one attains the infinite Bliss. How can the mind and senses grasp That which shines in the heart of all as the eternal Subject ? "

Totā Purī asked the disciple to withdraw his mind from all objects of the relative world, including the gods and goddesses, and to concentrate on the Absolute. But the task was not easy even for Sri Ramakrishna. He found it impossible to take his mind beyond Kāli, the divine mother of the universe. "After the initiation ", Sri Ramakrishna once said, describing the event, " Nāngtā began to teach me the various conclusions of the Advaita Vedanta and asked me to withdraw the mind completely from all objects and dive deep into the Ātman. But in spite of all my attempts, I could not altogether cross the realm of name and form and bring my mind to the unconditioned state. I had no difficulty in taking the mind from all the objects of the world. But the radiant and too familiar figure of the blissful Mother, the Embodiment of the essence of pure consciousness, appeared before me as a living reality. Her bewitching smile prevented me from passing into the great Beyond. Again and again I tried, but She stood in my way every time. In despair I said to Nāngtā : "It is hopeless. I cannot raise my mind to the unconditioned state and come face to face with Ātman.' He grew excited and sharply said : 'What ? You can't do it ? But you have to.' He cast his eyes around. Finding a piece of glass he took it up and stuck it between my eyebrows. ' Concentrate the mind on this point !' he thundered. Then with stern determination I again sat to meditate. As soon as the gracious form of the divine Mother appeared before me, I used my discrimination as a sword and with it clove Her in two. The last barrier fell. My spirit at once soared beyond the relative plane and I lost myself in samādhi."

Sri Ramakrishna remained completely absorbed in samādhi for three days. "Is it really true?" Totā Purī cried out in astonishment. " Is it possible that he has attained in a single day what it took me forty years of strenuous practice to achieve ? Great God ! It is nothing short of a miracle !" With the help of Totā Purī, Sri Ramakrishna's mind finally came down to the relative plane.

Totā Purī, a monk of the most orthodox type, never stayed at a place more than three days. But he remained at Dakshineswar eleven months. He too had something to learn.

Totā Purī had no idea of the struggles of ordinary men in the toils of passion and desire. Having maintained all through life the guilelessness of a child, he laughed at the idea of a man's being led astray by the senses. He was convinced that the world was māyā and had only to be denounced to vanish for ever. A born non-dualist, he had no faith in a personal God. He did not believe in the terrible aspect of Kāli, much less in Her benign aspect. Music and the chanting of God's holy name were to him only so much nonsense. He ridiculed the spending of emotion on the worship of a personal God.

KĀLI AND MĀYĀ

Sri Ramakrishna, on the other hand, though fully aware, like his guru, that the world is an illusory appearance, instead on slighting māyā, like an orthodox monist, acknowledged its power in the relative life. He was all love and reverence for māyā, perceiving in it a mysterious and majestic expression of Divinity. To him māyā itself was God, for everything was God. It was one of the faces of Brahman. What he had realized on the heights of the transcendental plane, he also found here below, everywhere about him, under the mysterious garb of names and forms. And this garb was a perfectly transparent sheath, through which he recognized the glory of the divine Immanence. Māyā, the mighty weaver of the garb, is none other than Kāli, the divine Mother. She is the primordial divine Energy, Sakti, and she can no more be distinguished from the supreme Brahman than can the power of burning be distinguished from fire. She projects the world and again withdraws it. She spins it as the spider spins its web. She is the Mother of the Universe, identical with the Brahman of Vedanta, and with the Ātman of Yoga. As eternal law-giver, She makes and unmakes laws; it is by Her imperious will that karma yields its fruit. She ensnares men with illusion and again releases them from bondage with a look of Her benign eyes. She is the supreme Mistress of the cosmic play, and all objects, animate and inanimate, dance by Her will. Even those who realize the Absolute in nirvikalpa samādhi are under Her jurisdiction as long as they live on the relative plane.

Thus, after nirvikalpa samādhi, Sri Ramakrishna realized māyā in an altogether new role. The binding aspect of Kāli vanished from before his vision. She no longer obscured his understanding. The world became the glorious manifestation of the divine Mother. Māyā became Brahman. The transcendental Itself broke through the Immanent. Sri Ramakrishna discovered that māyā operates in the relative world in two ways, and he termed these "avidyā-māyā" and "vidyā-māyā". Avidyā-māyā represents the dark forces of creation : sensuous desires, evil passions, greed, lust, cruelty, and so on. It sustains the world system on the lower planes. It is responsible for the round of man's birth and death. It must be fought and vanquished. But vidyā-māyā is the higher orce of creation : the spiritual virtues, the enlightening qualities, kindness, purity, love, devotion. Vidyā-māyā elevates man to the higher planes of consciousness. With the help of vidyā-māyā the devotee rids himself of avidyā-māyā ; he then becomes māyātīta, free of māyā. The two aspects of māyā are the two forces of creation, the two powers of Kāli ; and She stands beyond them both. She is like the effulgent sun, bringing into existence and shining through and standing behind the clouds of different colours and shapes, conjuring up wonderful forms in the blue autumn heaven.

The divine Mother asked Sri Ramakrishna not to be lost in the featureless Absolute but to remain in bhāvamukha, on the threshold of relative consciousness, the border line between the Absolute and the Relative. He was to keep himself at the "sixth centre" of Tantra, from which he could see not only the glory of the seventh, but also the divine manifestations of the Kundalini in the lower centres. He gently oscillated back and forth across the dividing line. Ecstatic devotion to the divine Mother alternated with serene absorption in the ocean of absolute Unity. He thus bridged the gulf between the personal and the impersonal, the immanent and the transcendent aspects of Reality. This is a unique experience in the recorded spiritual history of the world.

TOTĀ PURĪ'S LESSON

From Sri Ramakrishna Totā Purī had to learn the significance of Kāli, the great fact of the relative world, and of māyā, Her indescribable power.

One day, when guru and disciple were engaged in an animated discussion about Vedānta, a servant of the temple garden came there and took a coal from the sacred fire that had been lighted by the great ascetic. He wanted it to light his tobacco. Totā Purī flew into a rage and was about to beat the man. Sri Ramakrishna rocked with laughter. " What a shame ! " he cried. " You are explaining to me the reality of Brahman and the illusoriness of the world; yet now you have so far forgotten yourself as to be about to beat a man in a fit of passion. The power of māyā is indeed inscrutable !" Totā Purī was embarrassed.

About this time Totā Purī was suddenly laid up with a severe attack of dysentery. On account of this miserable illness he found it impossible to meditate. One night the pain became excruciating. He could no longer concentrate on Brahman. The body stood in the way. He became incensed with its demands. A free soul, he did not at all care for the body. So he determined to drown it in the Ganges. Thereupon he walked into the river. But, lo ! He walks to the other bank.[5] Is there not enough water in the Ganges ? Standing dumbfounded on the other bank he looks back across the water. The trees, the temples, the houses, are silhouetted against the sky. Suddenly, in one dazzling moment, he sees on all sides the presence of the divine Mother. She is in everything; She is everything. She is in

---

[5] This version of the incident is taken from the biography of Sri Ramakrishna *viz.*, SRI RAMAKRISHNA THE GREAT MASTER by Swami Saradananda, one of the Master's direct disciples.

the water; She is on land. She is the body: She is the mind. She is pain; She is comfort. She is knowledge; She is ignorance, She is life; She is death. She is everything that one sees, hears, or imagines. She turns "yea" into "nay", and "nay" into "yea". Without Her grace no embodied being can go beyond Her realm. Man has no free will. He is not even free to die. Yet, again, beyond the body and mind She resides in Her transcendental, absolute aspect. She is the Brahman that Totā Purī had been worshipping all his life.

Totā Purī returned to Dakshineswar and spent the remaining hours of the night meditating on the divine Mother. In the morning he went to the Kāli temple with Sri Ramakrishna and prostrated himself before the image of the Mother. He now realized why he had spent eleven months at Dakshineswar. Bidding farewell to the disciple, he continued on his way, enlightened.

Sri Ramakrishna later described the significance of Totā Purī's lessons: "When I think of the supreme Being as inactive—neither creating nor preserving nor destroying—, I call Him Brahman or Purusha, the impersonal God. When I think of Him as active—creating, preserving, and destroying—, I call Him S'akti or māyā or prakriti, the personal God. But the distinction between them does not mean a difference. The personal and the impersonal are the same thing, like milk and its whiteness, the diamond and its lustre, the snake and its wriggling motion. It is impossible to conceive of the one without the other. The divine Mother and Brahman are one."

After the departure of Totā Purī, Sri Ramakrishna remained for six months in a state of absolute identity with Brahman. "For six months at a stretch", he said, "I remained in that state from which ordinary men can never return; generally the body falls off, after three weeks, like a sere leaf. I was not conscious of day and night.. Flies would enter my mouth and nostrils just as they do a dead body's, but I did not feel them. My hair became matted with dust."

His body would not have survived but for the kindly attention of a monk who happened to be at Dakshineswar at that time and who somehow realized that for the good of humanity Sri Ramakrishna's body must be preserved. He tried various means, even physical violence, to recall the fleeing soul to the prison-house of the body, and during the resultant fleeting moments of consciousness he would push a few morsels of food down Sri Ramakrishna's throat. Presently Sri Ramakrishna received the command of the divine Mother to remain on the threshold of relative consciousness. Soon thereafter he was afflicted with a serious attack of dysentery. Day and night the pain tortured him, and his mind gradually came down to the physical plane.

CHAPTER IV

THE MASTER IN THE MAKING

FROM now on Sri Ramakrishna began to seek the company of devotees and holy men. He had gone through the storm and stress of spiritual disciplines and visions. Now he realized an inner calmness and appeared to others as a normal person. But he could not bear the company of worldly people or listen to their talk. Fortunately the holy atmosphere of Dakshineswar and the liberality of Mathur attracted monks and holy men from all parts of the country. Sādhus of all denominations—monists and dualists, Vaishnavas and Vedāntists, S'aktas and worshippers of Rama—flocked there in ever-increasing numbers. Ascetics and visionaries came to seek Sri Ramakrishna's advice. Vaishnavas had come during the period of his Vaishnava sādhanā, and Tāntriks when he practised the disciplines of Tantra. Vedāntists began to arrive after the departure of Totā Purī. In the room of Sri Ramakrishna, who was then in bed with dysentery, the Vedāntists engaged in scriptural discussions, and forgetting his own physical suffering, he solved their doubts by referring directly to his own experiences. Many of the visitors were genuine spiritual souls, the unseen pillars of Hinduism and their spiritual lives were quickened in no small measure by the sage of Dakshineswar. Sri Ramakrishna in turn learnt from them anecdotes concerning the ways and the conduct of holy men, which he subsequently narrated to his devotees and disciples. At his request Mathur provided him with large stores of food-stuffs, clothes and so forth, for distribution among the wandering monks.

Sri Ramakrishna had not read books, yet he possessed an encyclopedic knowledge of religions and religious philosophies. This he acquired from his contacts with innumerable holy men and scholars. He had a unique power of assimilation; through meditation he made this knowledge a part of his being. Once, when he was asked by a disciple about the source of his seemingly inexhaustible knowledge, he replied: " I have not read ; but I have heard the learned. I have made a garland of their knowledge, wearing it round my neck and I have given it as an offering at the feet of the Mother."

Sri Ramakrishna used to say that when the flower blooms the bees come to it for honey of their own accord. Now many souls began to visit Dakshineswar to satisfy their spiritual hunger. He, the devotee and aspirant, became the Master. Gauri, the great scholar who had been one of the first to proclaim Sri Ramakrishna an Incarnation of God, paid the Master a visit in 1870 and with the Master's blessings renounced the world. Nārāyan Shāstrī, another great pundit, who had mastered the six systems of Hindu philosophy and had been offered a lucrative post by the Mahārājā of Jaipur, met the Master and recognised in him one who had realized in life those ideals which he himself had encountered merely in books. Sri Ramakrishna initiated Nārāyan Shāstrī, at his earnest request, into the life of sannyās. Pundit Padmalochan, the court pundit of the Mahārājā of Burdwān, well known for his scholarship in both the Vedānta and the Nyāya systems of philosophy, accepted the Master as an Incarnation of God. Krishnakishore, a Vedāntist scholar, became devoted to the Master. And there arrived Viswanāth Upādhyāya, who was to become a favourite devotee ; Sri Ramakrishna always addressed him as " Captain". He was a high officer of the king of Nepal and had received the title of Colonel in recognition of his merit. A scholar of the *Gita*, the *Bhāgavata* and the Vedānta philosophy, he daily performed the worship of his chosen Deity with great devotion. " I have read the Vedas and the other scriptures ", he said. " I have also met a good many monks and devotees in different places. But it is in Sri Ramakrishna's presence that my spiritual yearnings have been fulfilled. To me he seems to be the embodiment of the truths of the scriptures."

The knowledge of Brahman in nirvikalpa samādhi had convinced Sri Ramakrishna that the gods of the different religions are but so many readings of the Absolute, and that the ultimate Reality could never be expressed by human tongue. He understood that all religions lead their devotees by differing paths to one and the same goal. Now he became eager to explore some of the alien religions; for with him understanding meant actual experience.

ISLĀM

Toward the end of 1866 he began to practise the disciplines of Islām. Under the direction of his Mussalmān guru he abandoned himself to his new sādhanā. He dressed as a Mussalmān and repeated the name of Āllāh. His prayers took the form of the Islāmic devotions. He forgot the Hindu gods and goddesses—even Kāli—and gave up visiting the temples. He took up his residence outside the temple precincts. After three days he saw the vision of a radiant figure, perhaps Mohammed. This figure gently approached him and finally lost himself in Sri Ramakrishna. Thus he realized the Mussalmān God. Thence he passed into communion with Brahman. The mighty river of Islām also led him back to the ocean of the Absolute.

CHRISTIANITY

Eight years later, some time in November, 1874, Sri Ramakrishna was seized with an irresistible desire to learn the truth of the Christian religion. He began to listen to readings from the Bible, by S'ambhucharan Mallick, a gentleman of Calcutta and

a devotee of the Master. Sri Ramakrishna became fascinated by
the life and teachings of Jesus. One day he was seated in the
parlour of Jadu Mallick's garden house[6] at Dakshineswar, when
his eyes became fixed on a painting of the Madonna and Child
Intently watching it, he became gradually overwhelmed with
divine emotion. The figures in the picture took on life, and the
rays of light emanating from them entered his soul. The effect of
this experience was stronger than that of the vision of Mohammed.
In dismay he cried out; "O Mother! What are you doing to
me?" And, breaking through the barriers of creed and religion,
he entered a new realm of ecstasy. Christ possessed his soul.
For three days he did not set foot in the Kāli temple. On the
fourth day, in the afternoon, as he was walking in the Panchavatī,
he saw coming toward him a person with beautiful large eyes,
serene countenance and fair skin. As the two faced each other,
a voice rang out in the depths of Sri Ramakrishna's soul:
"Behold the Christ, who shed His heart's blood for the redemption
of the world, who suffered a sea of anguish for love of men. It is
He, the master Yogi, who is in eternal union with God. It is
Jesus, love Incarnate." The Son of Man embraced the Son of
the divine Mother and merged in him. Sri Ramakrishna
realized his identity with Christ, as he had already realized his
identity with Kāli, Rama, Hanumān, Rādhā, Krishna, Brahman,
and Mohammed. The Master went into samādhi and communed
with the Brahman with attributes. Thus he experienced the
truth that Christianity, too, was a path leading to God-
consciousness. Till the last moment of his life he believed that
Christ was an Incarnation of God. But Christ, for him, was not
the only Incarnation; there were others—Buddha, for instance,
and Krishna.

---

6 This expression is used throughout to translate the Bengali word
denoting a rich man's country house set in a garden.

ATTITUDE TOWARD DIFFERENT RELIGIONS

Sri Ramakrishna accepted the divinity of Buddha and used to point out the similarity of his teachings to those of the Upanishads. He also showed great respect for the Tīrthankaras, who founded Jainism, and for the ten Gurus of S'ikhism. But he did not speak of them as divine Incarnations. He was heard to say that the Gurus of S'ikhism were the reincarnations of king Janaka of ancient India. He kept in his room at Dakshineswar a small statue of Tīrthankara Mahāvīra and a picture of Christ, before which incense was burnt morning and evening.

Without being formally initiated into their doctrines, Sri Ramakrishna thus realized the ideals of religions other than Hinduism. He did not need to follow any doctrine. All barriers were removed by his overwhelming love of God. So he became a Master who could speak with authority regarding the ideas and ideals of the various religions of the world. " I have practised ", said he, "all religions—Hinduism, Islām, Christianity—and I have also followed the paths of the different Hindu sects. I have found that it is the same God toward whom all are directing their steps, though along different paths. You must try all beliefs and traverse all the different ways once. Wherever I look, I see men quarrelling in the name of religion—Hindus, Mohammedans, Brāhmos, Vaishnavas and the rest. But they never reflect that He who is called Krishna is also called S'iva, and bears the name of the primal Energy, Jesus and Allāh as well—the same Rama with a thousand names. A lake has several ghāts. At one the Hindus take water in pitchers and call it ' jal'; at another the Mussalmāns take water in leather bags and call it ' pāni '; at a third the Christians call it 'water'. Can we imagine that it is not ' jal ', but only ' pāni ' or ' water '? How ridiculous! The substance is One under different names, and everyone is seeking the same substance; only climate,

R—5

temperament and name create differences. Let each man follow his own path. If he sincerely and ardently wishes to know God, peace be unto him! He will surely realize Him."

In 1867 Sri Ramakrishna returned to Kāmārpukur to recuperate from the effect of his austerities. The peaceful countryside, the simple and artless companions of his boyhood, and the pure air did him much good. The villagers were happy to get back their playful, frank, witty, kind-hearted, and truthful Gadādhar, though they did not·fail to notice the great change that had come over him during his years in Calcutta. His wife, Sāradā Devī, now fourteen years old, soon arrived at Kāmār-pukur. Her spiritual development was much beyond her age and she was able to understand immediately her husband's state of mind. She became eager to learn from him about God and to live with him as his attendant. The Master accepted her cheerfully both as his disciple and as his spiritual companion. Referring to the experiences of these few days, she once said: "I used to feel always as if a pitcher full of bliss were placed in my heart. The joy was indescribable."

PILGRIMAGE

On January 27, 1868, Mathur Bābu with a party of some one hundred and twenty-five persons set out on a pilgrimage to the sacred places of northern India. At Vaidyanāth in Behar, when the Master saw the inhabitants of a village reduced by poverty and starvation to mere skeletons, he requested his rich patron to feed the people and give each a piece of cloth. Mathur demurred at the added expense. The Master declared bitterly that he would not go on to Bānārās, but would live with the poor and share their miseries. He actually left Mathur and sat down with the villagers. Whereupon Mathur had to yield. On another occasion, two years later, Sri Ramakrishna showed a similar sentiment for the poor and needy. He accompanied

Mathur on a tour to one of the latter's estates at the time of the collection of rents. For two years the harvests had failed and the tenants were in a state of extreme poverty. The Master asked Mathur to remit their rents, distribute help to them and in addition give the hungry people a sumptuous feast. When Mathur grumbled, the Master said: " You are only the steward of the divine Mother. They are the Mother's tenants. You must spend the Mother's money. When they are suffering, how can you refuse to help them? You must help them." Again Mathur had to give in. Sri Ramakrishna's sympathy for the poor sprang from his perception of God in all created beings. His sentiment was not that of the humanist or philanthropist. To him the service of man was the same as the worship of God.

The party entered holy Bānārās by boat along the Ganges. When Sri Ramakrishna's eyes fell on this city of S'iva, where had accumulated for ages the devotion and piety of countless worshippers, he saw it to be made of gold, as the scriptures declare. He was visibly moved. During his stay in the city he treated every particle of its earth with utmost respect. At the Manikarnikā Ghāt, the great cremation ground of the city, he actually saw S'iva, with ash-covered body and tawny matted hair, serenely approaching each funeral pyre and breathing into the ears of the corpses the mantra of liberation; and then the divine Mother removing from the dead their bonds. Thus he realized the significance of the scriptural statement that anyone dying in Bānārās attains salvation through the grace of S'iva. He paid a visit to Trailanga Swami, the celebrated monk, whom he later declared to be a real paramahamsa, a veritable image of S'iva.

Sri Ramakrishna visited Allāhābād, at the confluence of the Ganges and the Jamunā and then proceeded to Vrindāvan and Mathurā, hallowed by the legends, songs, and dramas about

Krishna and the gopis. Here he had numerous visions and his heart overflowed with divine emotion. He wept and said: "O Krishna! Everything here is as it was in the olden days. You alone are absent." He visited the great woman saint, Gangāmāyī, regarded by Vaishnava devotees as the reincarnation of an intimate attendant of Rādhā. She was sixty years old and had frequent trances. She spoke of Sri Ramakrishna as an incarnation of Rādhā. With great difficulty he was persuaded to leave her.

On the return journey Mathur wanted to visit Gayā, but Sri Ramakrishna declined to go. He recalled his father's vision at Gayā, before his own birth and felt that in the temple of Vishnu he would become permanently absorbed in God. Mathur, honouring the Master's wish, returned with his party to Calcutta.

From Vrindāvan the Master had brought a handful of dust. Part of this he scattered in the Panchavatī; the rest he buried in the little hut where he had practised meditation. "Now this place", he said, "is as sacred as Vrindāvan."

In 1870, the Master went on a pilgrimage to Nadīā, the birth-place of Sri Chaitanya. As the boat by which he travelled approached the sand-bank close to Nadīā, Sri Ramakrishna had a vision of the "two brothers", Sri Chaitanya and his companion Nityānanda, "bright as molten gold" and with haloes, rushing to greet him with uplifted hands. "There they come! There they come!" he cried. They entered his body and he went into a deep trance.

RELATION WITH HIS WIFE

In 1872, Sāradā Devī paid her first visit to her husband at Dakshineswar. Four years earlier she had seen him at Kāmārpukur and had tasted the bliss of his divine company. Since then she had become even more gentle, tender, introspective, serious, and unselfish. She had heard many rumours about her husband's insanity. People had shown her pity in her misfortune. The more she thought, the more she felt that her duty was to be with him, giving him, in whatever measure she could, a wife's devoted service. She was now eighteen years old. Accompanied by her father, she arrived at Dakshineswar, having come on foot the distance of eighty miles. She had had an attack of fever on the way. When she arrived at the temple garden the Master said sorrowfully: "Ah! You have come too late. My Mathur is no longer here to look after you." Mathur had passed away the previous year.

The Master took up the duty of instructing his young wife and this included everything from housekeeping to the knowledge of Brahman. He taught her how to trim a lamp, how to behave toward people according to their differing temperaments and how to conduct herself before visitors. He instructed her in the mysteries of spiritual life—prayer, meditation, japa, deep contemplation and samādhi. The first lesson that Sāradā Devī received was: "God is everybody's beloved, just as the moon is dear to every child. Everyone has the same right to pray to Him. Out of His grace He reveals Himself to all who call upon Him. You too will see Him if you but pray to Him."

Totā Purī, coming to know of the Master's marriage, had once remarked: "What does it matter? He alone is firmly established in the knowledge of Brahman who can adhere to his spirit of discrimination and renunciation even while living with his wife. He alone has attained the supreme illumination who can look on man and woman alike as Brahman. A man with the idea of sex may be a good aspirant, but he is still far from the goal." Sri Ramakrishna and his wife lived together at Dakshineswar, but their minds always soared above the worldly plane. A few months after Sāradā Devī's arrival Sri Ramakrishna arranged, on an auspicious day, a special worship of Kāli, the divine Mother. Instead of an image of the Deity, he placed on the seat the living image, Sāradā Devī herself. The worshipper and the worshipped went into deep samādhi and in the transcendental plane their souls were united. After several hours Sri Ramakrishna came down again to the relative plane, sang a hymn to the great Goddess and surrendered, at the feet of the living image, himself, his rosary, and the fruit of his life-long sādhanā. This is known in Tantra as the Shoras'ī Pujā, the "Adoration of Woman". Sri Ramakrishna realized the significance of the great statement of the Upanishad: "O Lord, Thou art the woman, Thou art the man; Thou art the boy, Thou art the girl; Thou art the old, tottering on their crutches. Thou pervadest the universe in its multiple forms."

By his marriage Sri Ramakrishna admitted the great value of marriage in man's spiritual evolution, and by adhering to his monastic vows he demonstrated the imperative necessity of self-control, purity and continence, in the realization of God. By his unique spiritual relationship with his wife he proved that husband and wife can live together as spiritual companions. Thus his life is a synthesis of the ways of life of the householder and the monk.

THE "EGO" OF THE MASTER

In the nirvikalpa samādhi Sri Ramakrishna had realized that Brahman alone is real and the world illusory. By keeping his mind six months on the plane of the non-dual Brahman, he had attained to the state of the vijnānī, the knower of truth in a special and very rich sense, who sees Brahman not only in himself and in the transcendental Absolute, but in everything of the world. In this state of vijnāna, sometimes, bereft of body-consciousness, he would regard himself as one with Brahman; sometimes, conscious of the dual world, he would regard himself as God's devotee, servant, or child. In order to enable the Master to work for the welfare of humanity, the divine Mother had kept in him a trace of ego, which he described—according to his mood—as the "ego of knowledge", the "ego of devotion", the ego of a child ", or the " ego of a servant". In any case this ego of the Master consumed by the fire of the knowledge of Brahman, was an appearance only, like a burnt string. He often referred to this ego as the "ripe ego" in contrast with the ego of the bound soul, which he described as the "unripe" or "green" ego. The ego of the bound soul identifies itself with the body, relatives, possessions, and the world; but the "ripe ego", illumined by divine knowledge, knows the body, relatives, possessions and the world to be unreal and establishes a relationship of love with God alone. Through this "ripe ego" Sri Ramakrishna dealt with the world and his wife. One day, while stroking his feet, Sāradā Devī asked the Master, "What do you think of me?" Quick came the answer: "The Mother who is worshipped in the temple, is the mother who has given birth to my body and is now living in the nahabat and it is She again who is stroking my feet at this moment. Indeed, I always look on you as the personification of the blissful Mother Kāli."

Sāradā Devī, in the company of her husband, had rare spiritual experiences. She said: "I have no words to describe my wonderful exaltation of spirit as I watched him in his different moods. Under the influence of divine emotion he would sometimes talk on abstruse subjects, sometimes laugh, sometimes weep, and sometimes become perfectly motionless in samādhi. This would continue throughout the night. There was such an extraordinary divine presence in him that now and then I would shake with fear and wonder how the night would pass. Months went by in this way. Then one day he discovered that I had to keep awake the whole night lest, during my sleep, he should go into samādhi—for it might happen at any moment—, and so he asked me to sleep in the nahabat."

SUMMARY OF THE MASTER'S SPIRITUAL EXPERIENCES

We have now come to the end of Sri Ramakrishna's sādhanā, the period of his spiritual discipline. As a result of his supersensuous experiences he reached certain conclusions regarding himself and spirituality in general. His conclusions about himself may be summarized as follows :

First, he was an Incarnation of God, a specially commissioned person, whose spiritual experiences were for the benefit of humanity. Whereas it takes an ordinary man a whole life's struggle to realize one or two phases of God, he had in a few years realized God in all His phases.

Second, he knew that he had always been a free soul, that the various disciplines through which he had passed were really not necessary for his own liberation but were solely for the benefit of others. Thus the terms liberation and bondage were not applicable to him. As long as there are beings who consider themselves bound, God must come down to earth as an Incarnation to free them from bondage, just as a magistrate must visit any part of his district in which there is trouble.

Third, he came to foresee the time of his death. His words with respect to this matter were literally fulfilled.

About spirituality in general the following were his conclusions :

First, he was firmly convinced that all religions are true, that every doctrinal system represents a path to God. He had followed all the main paths and all had led him to the same goal. He was the first religious prophet recorded in history to preach the harmony of religions.

Second, the three great systems of thought known as Dualism, Qualified Non-dualism, and Absolute Non-dualism—Dvaita, Vis'ishtādvaita, and Advaita—he perceived to represent three stages in man's progress toward the ultimate Reality. They were not contradictory but complementary and suited to different temperaments. For the ordinary man with strong attachment to the senses, a dualistic form of religion, prescribing a certain amount of material support, such as music and other symbols, is useful. A man of God-realization transcends the idea of worldly duties, but the ordinary mortal must perform his duties, striving to be unattached and to surrender the results to God. The mind can comprehend and describe the range of thought and experience up to the Vis'ishtādvaita, and no further. The Advaita, the last word in spiritual experience, is something to be felt in samādhi, for it transcends mind and speech. From the highest standpoint, the Absolute and Its manifestation are equally real—the Lord's name, His abode, and the Lord Himself are of the same spiritual essence. Everything is spirit, the difference being only in form.

Third, Sri Ramakrishna realized the wish of the divine Mother that through him She should found a new Order, consisting of those who would uphold the universal doctrines illustrated in his life.

Fourth, his spiritual insight told him that those who were having their last birth on the mortal plane of existence and those who had sincerely called on the Lord even once in their lives must come to him.

During this period Sri Ramakrishna suffered several bereavements. The first was the death of a nephew named Akshay.

After the young man's death Sri Ramakrishna said: "Akshay died before my very eyes. But it did not affect me in the least. I stood by and watched a man die. It was like a sword being drawn from its scabbard. I enjoyed the scene, and laughed and sang and danced over it. They removed the body and cremated it. But the next day as I stood there (*pointing to the south-east verandah of his room*), I felt a racking pain for the loss of Akshay. as if somebody were squeezing my heart like a wet towel. I wondered at it and thought that the Mother was teaching me a lesson. I was not much concerned even with my own body— much less with a relative. But if such was my pain at the loss of a nephew, how much more must be the grief of the householders at the loss of their near and dear ones!" In 1871 Mathur died, and some five years later Sambhu Mallick—who, after Mathur's passing away, had taken care of the Master's comfort. In 1873 died his elder brother Rameswar, and in 1876, his beloved mother. These bereavements left their imprint on the tender human heart of Sri Ramakrishna, albeit he had realized the immortality of the soul and the illusoriness of birth and death.

In March 1875, about a year before the death of his mother, the Master met Keshabchandra Sen. The meeting was a momentous event for both Sri Ramakrishna and Keshab. Here the Master for the first time came into actual contact with a worthy representative of modern India.

BRĀHMO SAMĀJ

Keshab was the leader of the Brāhmo Samāj, one of the two great movements that, during the latter part of the nineteenth century, played an important part in shaping the course of the renaissance of India. The founder of the Brāhmo movement had been the great Rājā Rammohan Roy (1774—1833). Though born in an orthodox brāhmin family, Rammohan Roy had shown great sympathy for Islām and Christianity. He had gone to Tibet in search of the Buddhist mysteries. He had extracted from Christianity its ethical system, but had rejected the divinity of Christ as he had denied the Hindu Incarnations. The religion of Islām influenced him to a great extent, in the formulation of his monotheistic doctrines. But he always went back to the Vedas for his spiritual inspiration. The Brāhmo Samāj, which he founded in 1828, was dedicated to the " worship and adoration of the eternal, the unsearchable, the immutable Being, who is the author and preserver of the universe." The Samāj was open to all without distinction of colour, creed, caste, nation or religion.

The real organizer of the Samāj was Devendranāth Tāgore (1817–1905), the father of the poet Rabindranath. His physical and spiritual beauty, aristocratic aloofness, penetrating intellect, and poetic sensibility made him the foremost leader of the educated Bengalis. These addressed him by the respectful epithet of Maharshi, the "Great Seer". The Maharshi was a Sanskrit scholar and, unlike Rājā Rammohan Roy, drew his inspiration entirely from the Upanishads. He was an implacable enemy of image worship and also fought to stop the infiltration of Christian ideas into the Samāj. He gave the movement its faith and ritual. Under his influence the Brāhmo Samāj professed one self-existent supreme Being Who had created the universe out of nothing, the God of truth, infinite wisdom, goodness, and power, the Eternal and Omnipotent, the One without a second. Man should love Him and do His will, believe in Him and worship Him, and thus merit salvation in the world to come.

By far the ablest leader of the Brāhmo movement was Keshabchandra Sen (1838-1884). Unlike Rājā Rammohan Roy and Devendranāth Tāgore, Keshab was born of a middle-class Bengali family and had been brought up in an English school. He did not know Sanskrit and very soon broke away from the

popular Hindu religion. Even at an early age he came under the
spell of Christ and professed to have experienced the special
favour of John the Baptist, Christ, and St. Paul. When he
strove to introduce Christ to the Brāhmo Samāj, a rupture
became inevitable with Devendranāth. In 1868 Keshab broke
with the older leader and founded the Brāhmo Samāj of India,
Devendra retaining leadership of the first Brāhmo Samāj, now
called the Ādi Samāj.

Keshab possessed a complex nature. When passing through
a great moral crisis, he spent much of his time in solitude and
felt that he heard the voice of God. When a devotional form of
worship was introduced into the Brāhmo Samāj, he spent hours
in singing kīrtan with his followers. He visited England in 1870
and impressed the English people with his musical voice, his
simple English and his spiritual fervour. He was entertained by
Queen Victoria. Returning to India, he founded centres of the
Brāhmo Samāj in various parts of the country. Not unlike a
professor of comparative religion in a European university, he
began to discover, about the time of his first contact with Sri
Ramakrishna, the harmony of religions. He became sympathetic
toward the Hindu gods and goddesses, explaining them in a
liberal fashion. Further, he believed that he was called by God
to dictate to the world, God's newly revealed law, the New
Dispensation, the Navavidhān.

In 1878, a schism divided Keshab's Samāj. Some of his
influential followers accused him of infringing the Brāhmo principles by marrying his daughter to a wealthy man before she had
attained the marriageable age approved by the Samāj. This
group seceded and established the Sādhāran Brāhmo Samāj,
Keshab remaining the leader of the Navavidhān. Keshab now
began to be drawn more and more toward the Christ ideal
though under the influence of Sri Ramakrishna his devotion to

the divine Mother also deepened. His mental oscillation between Christ and the divine Mother of Hinduism found no position of rest. In Bengal and some other parts of India the Brāhmo movement took the form of unitarian Christianity, scoffed at Hindu rituals, and preached a crusade against image worship. Influenced by Western culture, it declared the supremacy of reason, advocated the ideals of the French Revolution, abolished the caste-system among its own members, stood for the emancipation of women, agitated for the abolition of early marriage, sanctioned the remarriage of widows and encouraged various educational and social reform movements. The immediate effect of the Brāhmo movement in Bengal was the checking of the proselytizing activities of the Christian missionaries. It also raised Indian culture in the estimation of its English masters. But it was an intellectual and eclectic religious ferment born of the necessity of the time. Unlike Hinduism, it was not founded on the deep inner experiences of sages and prophets. Its influence was confined to a comparatively few educated men and women of the country, and the vast masses of the Hindus remained outside it. It sounded monotonously only one of the notes in the rich gamut of the eternal religion of the Hindus.

ĀRYA SAMĀJ

The other movement playing an important part in the nineteenth-century religious revival of India was the Ārya Samāj. The Brāhmo Samāj, essentially a movement of compromise with European culture, tacitly admitted the superiority of the West. But the founder of the Ārya Samāj was a pugnacious Hindu sannyāsī who accepted the challenge of Islām and Christianity and was resolved to combat all foreign influence in India. Swami Dayānanda (1824-1883) launched this movement in Bombay in 1875, and soon its influence was felt throughout western India. The Swami was a great scholar of the Vedas, which he explained as being strictly monotheistic. He preached against the worship of images and re-established the ancient Vedic sacrificial rites. According to him the Vedas were the ultimate authority on religion and he accepted every word of them as literally true. The Ārya Samāj became a bulwark against the encroachments of Islām and Christianity, and its orthodox flavour appealed to many Hindu minds. It also assumed leadership in many movements of social reform. The caste-system became a target of its attack. Women it liberated from many of their social disabilities. The cause of education received from it a great impetus. It started agitation against early marriage and advocated the remarriage of Hindu widows. Its influence was strongest in the Punjab, the battle-ground of the Hindu and Islāmic cultures. A new fighting attitude was introduced into the slumbering Hindu society. Unlike the Brāhmo Samāj, the influence of the Arya Samāj was not confined to the intellectuals. It was a force that spread to the masses. It was a dogmatic movement intolerant of those who disagreed with its views and it emphasized only one way, the Ārya Samāj way, to the realization of Truth. Sri Ramakrishna met Swami Dayānanda when the latter visited Bengal.

KESHABCHANDRA SEN

Keshabchandra Sen and Sri Ramakrishna met for the first time in the garden house of Jaygopāl Sen at Belghariā, a few miles from Dakshineswar, where the great Brāhmo leader was staying with some of his disciples. In many respects the two were poles apart, though an irresistible inner attraction was to make them intimate friends. The Master had realized God as pure spirit and consciousness, but he believed in the various forms of God as well. Keshab, on the other hand, regarded image-worship as idolatry and gave allegorical explanations of the Hindu deities. Keshab was an orator and a writer of books and magazine articles ; Sri Ramakrishna had a horror of lecturing and hardly knew how to write his own name. Keshab's fame spread far and wide, even reaching the distant shores of England ; the Master still led a secluded life in the village of Dakshineswar. Keshab emphasized social reforms for India's regeneration ; to Sri Ramakrishna God-realization was the only goal of life. Keshab considered himself a disciple of Christ and accepted in a diluted form the Christian sacraments and Trinity ; Sri Ramakrishna was the simple child of Kāli, the divine Mother, though he too, in a different way, acknowledged Christ's divinity. Keshab was a house-holder and took a real interest in the welfare of his children, whereas Sri Ramakrishna was a Paramahamsa and completely indifferent to the life of the world. Yet, as their acquaintance ripened into friendship, Sri Ramakrishna and Keshab held each other in great love and respect. Years later, at the news of Keshab's death, the Master felt as if half his body had become paralyzed. Keshab's concepts of the harmony of religions and the Motherhood of God were deepened and enriched by his contact with Sri Ramakrishna.

Sri Ramakrishna, dressed in red-bordered dhoti, one end of which was carelessly thrown over his left shoulder, came to Jaygopāl's garden house accompanied by Hriday. No one took notice of the unostentatious visitor. Finally the Master said to Keshab, " People tell me you have seen God ; so I have come to hear from you about God. " A magnificent conversation followed. The Master sang a thrilling song about Kāli and forthwith went into samādhi. When Hriday uttered the sacred " Om " in his ears, he gradually came back to consciousness of the world, his face still radiating a divine brilliance. Keshab and his followers were amazed. The contrast between Sri Ramakrishna and the Brāhmo devotees was very interesting. There sat this small man, thin and extremely delicate. His eyes were illumined with an inner light. Good humour gleamed in his eyes and lurked in the corners of his mouth. His speech was Bengali of a homely kind with a slight, delightful stammer and his words held men enthralled by their wealth of spiritual experience, their inexhaustible store of simile and metaphor, their power of observation, their bright and subtle humour, their wonderful catholicity, their ceaseless flow of wisdom. And around him now were the sophisticated men of Bengal the best products of Western education, with Keshab, the idol of young Bengal, as their leader.

Keshab's sincerity was enough for Sri Ramakrishna. Henceforth the two saw each other frequently, either at Dakshineswar or at the temple of the Brāhmo Samāj. Whenever the Master was in the temple at the time of divine service, Keshab would request him to speak to the congregation. And Keshab would visit the saint, in his turn, with offerings of flowers and fruits.

OTHER BRĀHMO LEADERS

Gradually other Brāhmo leaders began to feel Sri Ramakrishna's influence. But they were by no means uncritical admirers of the Master. They particularly disapproved of his ascetic renunciation and condemnation of "woman and gold". They measured him according to their own ideals of the householder's life. Some could not understand his samādhi and described it as a nervous malady. Yet they could not resist his magnetic personality.

Among the Brāhmo leaders who knew the Master closely, were Pratāpchandra Mazumdār, Vijaykrishna Goswāmī, Trailokyanāth Sānnyāl and Shivanāth Shāstrī.

Shivanāth, one day, was greatly impressed by the Master's utter simplicity and abhorrence of praise. He was seated with

Sri Ramakrishna in the latter's room when several rich men of Calcutta arrived. The Master left the room for a few minutes. In the mean time Hriday, his nephew, began to describe his samādhi to the visitors. The last few words caught the Master's ear as he entered the room. He said to Hriday: " What a mean-spirited fellow you must be to extol me thus before these rich men! You have seen their costly apparel and their gold watches and chains and your object is to get from them as much money as you can. What do I care about what they think of me? (*Turning to the gentlemen*) No, my friends, what he has told you about me is not true. It was not love of God that made me absorbed in God and indifferent to external life. I became positively insane for some time. The sādhus who frequented this temple told me to practise many things. I tried to follow them and the consequence was that my austerities drove me to insanity." This is a quotation from one of Shivanāth's books. He took the Master's words literally and failed to see their real import.

Shivanāth vehemently criticized the Master for his other-worldly attitude toward his wife. He writes: " Ramakrishna was practically separated from his wife, who lived in her village home. One day when I was complaining to some friends about the virtual widowhood of his wife, he drew me to one side and whispered in my ear: ' Why do you complain? It is no longer possible; it is all dead and gone.' Another day as I was inveighing against this part of his teaching, and also declaring that our programme of work in the Brāhmo Samāj includes women, that ours is a social and domestic religion and that we want to give education and social liberty to women, the saint became very much excited, as was his way when anything against his settled conviction was asserted—a trait we so much liked in him—and exclaimed, ' Go, thou fool, go and perish in the pit that your

R—6

women will dig for you.' Then he glared at me and said: 'What does a gardener do with a young plant? Does he not surround it with a fence to protect it from goats and cattle? And when the young plant has grown up into a tree and it can no longer be injured by cattle, does he not remove the fence and let the tree grow freely?' I replied, 'Yes, that is the custom with gardeners.' Then he remarked, 'Do the same in your spiritual life; become strong, be full-grown; then you may seek them.' To which I replied, 'I don't agree with you in thinking that women's work is like that of cattle, destructive; they are our associates and helpers in our spiritual struggles and social progress — a view with which he could not agree and he marked his dissent by shaking his head. Then referring to the lateness of the hour he jocularly remarked, 'It is time for you to depart; take care, do not be late; otherwise *your woman* will not admit you into her room.' This evoked hearty laughter.''

Pratāpchandra Mazumdar, the right-hand man of Keshab and an accomplished Brāhmo preacher in Europe and America, bitterly criticized Sri Ramakrishna's use of uncultured language and also his austere attitude toward his wife. But he could not escape the spell of the Master's personality. In the course of an article about Sri Ramakrishna, Pratāp wrote in the 'Theistic Quarterly Review': "What is there in common between him and me? I, a Europeanized, civilized, self-centred, semi-sceptical, so-called educated reasoner, and he, a poor, illiterate, unpolished, half-idolatrous, friendless Hindu devotee? Why should I sit long hours to attend to him, I, who have listened to Disraeli and Fawcett, Stanley and Max Muller, and a whole host of European scholars and divines?...And it is not I only, but dozens like me, who do the same....He worships S'iva, he worships Kāli, he worships Rama, he worships Krishna and is a confirmed advocate of Vedāntic doctrines...He is an idolater, yet is a faithful and most devoted meditator on the perfections of the one formless, absolute infinite Deity....His religion is ecstasy, his worship means transcendental insight, his whole nature burns day and night with a permanent fire and fever of a strange faith and feeling....So long as he is spared to us, gladly shall we sit at his feet to learn from him the sublime precepts of purity, unworldliness, spirituality, and inebriation in the love of God.... He, by his childlike bhakti, by his strong conceptions of an ever-ready Motherhood, helped to unfold it [God as our Mother] in our minds wonderfully....By associating with him we learnt to realize better the divine attributes as scattered over the three hundred and thirty millions of deities of mythological India, the gods of the Purānas.''

The Brāhmo leaders received much inspiration from their contact with Sri Ramakrishna. It broadened their religious views and kindled in their hearts the yearning for God realization ; it made them understand and appreciate the rituals and symbols of Hindu religion, convinced them of the manifestation of God in diverse forms, and deepened their thoughts about the harmony of religions. The Master, too, was impressed by the sincerity of many of the Brāhmo devotees. He told them about his own realizations and explained to them the essence of his teachings, such as the necessity of renunciation, sincerity in the pursuit of one's own course of discipline, faith in God, the performance of one's duties without thought of results and descrimination between the real and the unreal.

This contact with the educated and progressive Bengalis opened Sri Ramakrishna's eyes to a new realm of thought. Born and brought up in a simple village, without any formal education, and taught by the orthodox holy men of India in religious life, he had had no opportunity to study the influence of modernism on the thoughts and lives of the Hindus. He could not properly estimate the result of the impact of Western education on Indian culture. He was a Hindu of the Hindus, renunciation being to him the only means to the realization of God in life. From the Brāhmos he learnt that the new generation of India made a compromise between God and the world. Educated young men were influenced more by the Western philosophers than by their own prophets. But Sri Ramakrishna was not dismayed, for he saw in this, too, the hand of God. And though he expounded to the Brāhmos all his ideas about God and austere religious disciplines, yet he bade them accept from his teachings only as much as suited their tastes and temperaments.

—oo⚬oo—

CHAPTER V
COMING OF DISCIPLES

CONTACT with the Brāhmos increased Sri Ramakrishna's longing to encounter aspirants who would be able to follow his teachings in their purest form. "There was no limit ", he once declared, " to the longing I felt at that time. During the day-time I somehow managed to control it. The secular talk of the worldly-minded was galling to me, and I would look wistfully to the day when my own beloved companions would come. I hoped to find solace in conversing with them and relating to them my own realizations. Every little incident would remind me of them, and thoughts of them wholly engrossed me. I was already arranging in my mind what I should say to one and give to another and so on. But when the day would come to a close I would not be able to curb my feelings. The thought that another day had gone by and they had not come, oppressed me. When, during the evening service, the temples rang with the sound of bells and conch-shells, I would climb to the roof of the kuthī in the garden and, writhing in anguish of heart, cry at the top of my voice: ' Come. my children! Oh, where are you? I cannot bear to live without you.' A mother never longed so intensely for the sight of her child, nor a friend for his companions, nor a lover for his sweetheart, as I longed for them. Oh, it was indescribable! Shortly after this period of yearning the devotees[7] began to come."

---

7 The word is generally used in the text to denote one devoted to God, a worshipper of the personal God, or a follower of the path of love A devotee of Sri Ramakrishna is one who is devoted to Sri Ramakrishna and follows his teachings. The word "disciple", when used in connexion with Sri Ramakrishna, refers to one who had been initiated into spiritual life by Sri Ramakrishna and who regarded him as his guru

In the year 1879 occasional writings about Sri Ramakrishna by the Brāhmos, in the Brāhmo magazines, began to attract his future disciples from the educated middle-class Bengalis and they continued to come till 1884. But others, too, came, feeling the subtle power of his attraction. They were an ever shifting crowd of people of all castes and creeds: Hindus and Brāhmos, Vaishnavas and S'āktas, the educated with university degrees and the illiterate, old and young, mahārājās and beggars, journalists and artists, pundits and devotees, philosophers and the worldly-minded, jnānis and yogīs, men of action and men of faith, virtuous women and prostitutes, officeholders and vagabonds, philanthropists and self-seekers, dramatists and drunkards, builders-up and pullers-down. He gave to them all, without stint, from his illimitable store of realization. No one went away empty-handed. He taught them the lofty knowledge of the Vedānta and the soul-melting love of the Purāna. Twenty hours out of twenty-four he would speak without rest or respite. He gave to all his sympathy and enlightenment and he touched them with that strange power of the soul which could not but melt even the most hardened. And people understood him according to their powers of comprehension.

THE MASTER'S METHOD OF TEACHING

But he remained as ever the willing instrument in the hand of God, the child of the divine Mother, totally untouched by the idea of being a teacher. He used to say that three ideas—that he was a guru, a father and a master—pricked his flesh like thorns. Yet he was an extraordinary teacher. He stirred his disciples' hearts more by a subtle influence than by actions or words. He never claimed to be the founder of a religion or the organizer of a sect. Yet he was a religious dynamo. He was the verifier of all religions and creeds. He was like an expert gardener, who prepares the soil and removes the weeds, knowing that the plants will grow because of the inherent power of the seeds, producing each its appropriate flowers and fruits. He never thrust his ideas on anybody. He understood people's limitations and worked on the principle that what is good for one may be bad for another. He had the unusual power of knowing the devotees' minds, even their inmost souls at the first sight. He accepted disciples with the full knowledge of their past tendencies and future possibilities. The life of evil did not frighten him, nor did religious squeamishness raise anybody in his estimation. He saw in everything the unerring finger of the divine Mother. Even the light that leads astray was to him the light from God.

To those who became his intimate disciples the Master was a friend, companion, and playmate. Even the chorers of religious discipline would be lightened in his presence. The devotees would be so inebriated with pure joy in his company that they would have no time to ask themselves whether he was an Incarnation, a perfect soul, or a yogī. His very presence was a great teaching; words were superfluous. In later years his disciples remarked that while they were with him they would regard him as a comrade, but afterwards would tremble to think of their frivolities in the presence of such a great person. They had convincing proof that the Master could, by his mere wish, kindle in their hearts the love of God and give them His vision.

Through all this fun and frolic, this merriment and frivolity, he always kept before them the shining ideal of God-consciousness and the path of renunciation. He prescribed ascents steep or graded according to the powers of the climber. He permitted no compromise with the basic principles of purity. An aspirant had to keep his body, mind, senses, and soul unspotted, had to have a sincere love for God and an ever mounting spirit of yearning. The rest would be done by the Mother.

His disciples were of two kinds the householders and the young men, some of whom were later to become monks. There was also a small group of women devotees.

HOUSEHOLDER DEVOTEES

For the householders Sri Ramakrishna did not prescribe the hard path of total renunciation. He wanted them to discharge their obligations to their families. Their renunciation was to be mental. Spiritual life could not be acquired by flying away from responsibilities. A married couple should live like brother and sister after the birth of one or two children, devoting their time to spiritual talk and contemplation. He encouraged the householders, saying that their life was, in a way, easier than that of the monk, since it was more advantageous to fight the enemy from inside a fortress than in an open field. He insisted, however, on their repairing into solitude every now and then to strengthen their devotion and faith in God through prayer, japa and meditation. He prescribed for them the companionship of sādhus. He asked them to perform their worldly duties with one hand, while holding to God with the other and to pray to God to make their duties fewer and fewer so that in the end they might cling to Him with both hands. He would discourage in both the householders and the celibate youths any lukewarmness in their spiritual struggles. He would not ask them to follow indiscriminately the ideal of non-resistance, which ultimately makes a coward of the unwary.

FUTURE MONKS

But to the young men destined to be monks he pointed out the steep path of renunciation, both external and internal. They must take the vow of absolute continence and eschew all thought of greed and lust. By the practice of continence, aspirants develop a subtle nerve through which they understand the deeper mysteries of God. For them self-control is final, imperative, and absolute. The sannyāsīs are teachers of men, and their lives should be totally free from blemish. They must not even look at a picture which may awaken their animal passions. The Master selected his future monks from young men untouched by " woman and gold " and plastic enough to be cast in his spiritual mould. When teaching them the path of renunciation and discrimination, he would not allow the householders to be anywhere near them.

RAM AND MANOMOHAN

The first two householder devotees to come to Dakshineswar were Ramchandra Dutta and Manomohan Mitra. A medical practitioner and chemist, Ram was sceptical about God and religion and never enjoyed peace of soul. He wanted tangible proof of God's existence. The Master said to him : " God really exists. You don't see the stars in the day-time, but that doesn't mean that the stars do not exist. There is butter in milk. But can anybody see it by merely looking at the milk ? To get butter you must churn milk in a quiet and cool place. You cannot realize God by a mere wish; you must go through some mental disciplines." By degrees the Master awakened Ram's spirituality and the latter became one of his foremost lay disciples. It was Ram who introduced Narendranāth to Sri Ramakrishna. Narendra was a relative of Ram.

Manomohan at first met with considerable opposition from his wife and other relatives, who resented his visits to Dakshineswar. But in the end the unselfish love of the Master triumphed over worldly affection. It was Manomohan who brought Rākhāl to the Master.

SURENDRA

Suresh Mitra, a beloved disciple whom the Master often addressed as Surendra, had received an English education and held an important post in an English firm. Like many other educated young men of the time, he prided himself on his atheism and led a Bohemian life. He was addicted to drinking. He cherished an exaggerated notion about man's free will. A victim of mental depression, he was brought to Sri Ramakrishna by Ramchandra Dutta. When he heard the Master asking a disciple to practise the virtue of self-surrender to God, he was impressed. But though he tried thence-forth to do so, he was unable to give up his old associates and his drinking. One day the Master said in his presence, "Well, when a man goes to an undesirable place, why doesn't he take the divine Mother with him?" And to Surendra himself Sri Ramakrishna said: "Why should you drink wine as wine? Offer it to Kāli, and then take it as Her prasād, as consecrated drink. But see that you don't become intoxicated; you must not reel and your thoughts must not wander. At first you will feel ordinary excitement, but soon you will experience spiritual exaltation." Gradually Surendra's entire life was changed. The Master designated him as one of those commissioned by the divine Mother to defray a great part of his expenses. Surendra's purse was always open for the Master's comfort.

KEDĀR

Kedārnāth Chatterji was endowed with a spiritual temperament and had tried various paths of religion, some not very commendable. When he met the Master at Dakshineswar he understood the true meaning of religion. It is said that the Master, weary of instructing devotees who were coming to him in great numbers for guidance, once prayed to the Goddess Kāli: "Mother, I am tired of speaking to people. Please give power to Kedār, Girish, Ram, Vijay, and Mahendra to give them the preliminary instruction, so that just a little teaching from me will be enough."

He was aware, however, of Kedār's lingering attachment to worldly things and often warned him about it.

HARISH

Harish, a young man in affluent circumstances, renounced his family and took shelter with the Master, who loved him for his sincerity, singleness of purpose, and quiet nature. He spent his leisure time in prayer and meditation, turning a deaf ear to the entreaties and threats of his relatives. Referring to his undisturbed peace of mind, the Master would say: "Real men are dead to the world though living. Look at Harish. He is an example." When one day the Master asked him to be a little kind to his wife, Harish said: "You must excuse me on this point. This is not the place to show kindness. If I try to be sympathetic to her, there is a possibility of my forgetting the ideal and becoming entangled in the world."

BHAVANĀTH

Bhavanāth Chātterji visited the Master while he was still in his teens. His parents and relatives regarded Sri Ramakrishna as an insane person and tried their utmost to prevent him from becoming intimate with the Master. But the young boy was very stubborn and often spent nights at Dakshineswar. He was greatly attached to Narendra and the Master encouraged their friendship. The very sight of him often awakened Sri Ramakrishna's spiritual emotion.

BALARĀM BOSE

Balarām Bose came of a wealthy Vaishnava family. From his youth he had shown a deep religious temperament and had devoted his time to meditation, prayer and the study of the Vaishnava scriptures. He was very much impressed by Sri Ramakrishna even at their first meeting. He asked Sri Ramakrishna whether God really existed and, if so, whether a man could realize Him. The Master said: "God reveals Himself to the devotee who thinks of Him as his nearest and dearest. Because you do not draw response by praying to Him once, you must not conclude that He does not exist. Pray to God, thinking of Him as dearer than your very self. He is much attached to His devotees. He comes to a man even before He is sought. There is none more intimate and affectionate than God." Balarām had never before heard God spoken of in such forceful words; every one of the words seemed true to him. Under the Master's influence he outgrew the conventions of the Vaishnava worship and became one of the most beloved of the disciples. It was at his home that the Master slept whenever he spent a night in Calcutta.

MAHENDRA OR M.

Mahendranāth Gupta, better known as " M.", arrived at Dakshineswar in March 1882. He belonged to the Brāhmo Samāj and was Headmaster of the Vidyāsāgar High School at S'yāmbāzār, Calcutta. At the very first sight the Master recognized him as one of his "marked" disciples. Mahendra recorded in his diary Sri Ramakrishna's conversations with his devotees. These are the first directly recorded words, in the spiritual history of the world, of a man recognized as belonging in the class of Buddha and Christ. Mahendra was instrumental, through his personal contacts, in spreading the Master's message among many young and aspiring souls.

NĀG MAHĀSHAY

Durgācharan Nāg, also known as Nāg Mahāshay, was the ideal house-holder among the lay disciples of Sri Ramakrishna. He was the embodiment of the Master's ideal of life in the world, unstained by worldliness. In spite of his intense desire to become a sannyāsī, Sri Ramakrishna asked him to live in the world in the spirit of a monk and the disciple truly carried out this injunction. He was born of a poor family and even during his boyhood often sacrificed everything to lessen the sufferings of the needy. He had married at an early age and after his wife's death had married a second time to obey his father's command. But he once said to his wife: "Love on the physical level never lasts. He is indeed blessed who can give his love to God with his whole heart. Even a little attachment to the body endures for several births. So do not be attached to this cage of bone and flesh. Take shelter at the feet of the Mother and think of Her alone. Thus your life here and hereafter will be ennobled." The Master spoke of him as a " blazing light ". He received every word of Sri Ramakrishna in dead earnest. One day he heard the Master saying that it was difficult for doctors, lawyers, and brokers to make much progress in spirituality. Of doctors he said, "If the mind clings to the tiny drops of medicine, how can it conceive of the Infinite ? " That was the end of Durgācharan's medical practice and he threw his chest of medicines into the Ganges. Sri Ramakrishna assured him that he would not lack simple food and clothing. He bade him serve holy men. On being asked where he would find real holy men, the Master said that the sādhus themselves would seek his company. No sannyāsī could have lived a more austere life than Durgācharan.

GIRISH GHOSH

Girishchandra Ghosh was a born rebel against God, a sceptic, a Bohemian, a drunkard. He was the greatest Bengali dramatist of his time, the father of the modern Bengali stage. Like other young men he had imbibed all the vices of the West. He had plunged into a life of dissipation and had become convinced that religion was only a fraud. Materialistic philosophy he justified as enabling one to get at least a little fun out of life. But a series of reverses shocked him and he became eager to solve the riddle of life. He had heard people say that in spiritual life the help of a guru was imperative and that the guru was to be regarded as God Himself. But Girish was too well acquainted with human nature to see perfection in a man. His first meeting with Sri Ramakrishna did not impress him at all. He returned home feeling as if he had seen a freak at a circus; for the Master, in a semi-conscious mood, had inquired whether it was evening, though the lamps were burning in the room. But their paths often crossed and Girish could not avoid further encounters. The Master attended a performance in Girish's Star Theatre. On this occasion, too, Girish found nothing impressive about him. One day, however, Girish happened to see the Master dancing and singing with the devotees. He felt the contagion and wanted to join them, but restrained himself for fear of ridicule. Another day Sri Ramakrishna was about to give him spiritual instruction, when Girish said: "I don't want to listen to instructions. I have myself written many instructions. They are of no use to me. Please help me in a more tangible way if you can." This pleased the Master and he asked Girish to cultivate faith.

As time passed, Girish began to learn that the guru is the one who silently unfolds the disciple's inner life. He became a steadfast devotee of the Master. He often loaded the Master with insults, drank in his presence and took liberties which astounded the other devotees. But the Master knew that at heart Girish was tender, faithful and sincere. He would not allow Girish to give up the theatre. And when a devotee asked him to tell Girish to give up drinking, he sternly replied: "That is none of your business. He who has taken charge of him will look after him. Girish is a devotee of heroic type. I tell you, drinking will not affect him." The Master knew that mere words could not induce a man to break deep-rooted habits, but that the silent influence of love worked miracles. Therefore he never asked him to give up alcohol, with the result that Girish himself eventually broke the habit. Sri Ramakrishna had strengthened Girish's resolution by allowing him to feel that he was absolutely free.

One day Girish felt depressed because he was unable to submit to any routine of spiritual discipline. In an exalted mood the Master said to him : "All right, give me your power of attorney. Henceforth I assume responsibility for you. You need not do anything." Girish heaved a sigh of relief. He felt happy to think that Sri Ramakrishna had assumed his spiritual responsibilities. But poor Girish could not then realize that he also, on his part, had to give up his freedom and make of himself a puppet in Sri Ramakrishna's hands. The Master began to discipline him according to this new attitude. One day Girish said about a trifling matter, "Yes, I shall do this." "No, no!" the Master corrected him. "You must not speak in that egotistic manner. You should say, 'God willing, I shall do it.'" Girish understood. Thenceforth he tried to give up all idea of personal responsibility and surrender himself to the divine will. His mind began to dwell constantly on Sri Ramakrishna. This unconscious meditation in time chastened his turbulent spirit.

The householder devotees generally visited Sri Ramakrishna on Sunday afternoons and other holidays. Thus a brotherhood was gradually formed, and the Master encouraged their fraternal feeling. Now and then he would accept an invitation to a devotee's home, where other devotees would also be invited. Kirtan would be arranged and they would spend hours in dance and devotional music. The Master would go into trances or open his heart in religious discourses and in the narration of his own spiritual experiences. Many people who could not go to

Dakshineswar participated in these meetings and felt blessed. Such an occasion would be concluded with a sumptuous feast.

But it was in the company of his younger devotees, pure souls yet unstained by the touch of worldliness, that Sri Ramakrishna took greatest joy. Among the young men who later embraced the householder's life were Nārāyan, Paltu, the younger Naren, Tejchandra and Pūrṇa. These visited the Master sometimes against strong opposition from home.

PŪRNA

Pūrṇa was a lad of thirteen, whom Sri Ramakrishna described as an Is'varakoti, a soul born with special spiritual qualities. The Master said that Pūrṇa was the last of the group of brilliant devotees who, as he once had seen in a trance, would come to him for spiritual illumination. Pūrṇa said to Sri Ramakrishna during their second meeting, " You are God Himself incarnated in flesh and blood." Such words coming from a mere youngster proved of what stuff the boy was made.

MAHIMĀCHARAN AND PRATĀP HĀZRĀ

Mahimācharan and Pratāp Hāzrā were two devotees outstanding for their pretentiousness and idiosyncrasies. But the Master showed them his unfailing love and kindness, though he was aware of their shortcomings. Mahimācharan Chakravarty had met the Master long before the arrival of the other disciples. He had had the intention of leading a spiritual life, but a strong desire to acquire name and fame was his weakness. He claimed to have been initiated by Totā Purā and used to say that he had been following the path of knowledge according to his guru's instructions. He possessed a large library of English and Sanskrit books. But though he pretended to have read them, most of the leaves were uncut. The Master knew all his limitations, yet enjoyed listening to him recite from the Vedas and other scriptures. He would always exhort Mahimā to meditate on the meaning of the scriptural texts and to practise spiritual discipline.

Pratāp Hāzrā, a middle-aged man, hailed from a village near Kāmārpukur. He was not altogether unresponsive to religious feelings. On a moment's impulse he had left his home, aged mother, wife and children and had found shelter in the temple-garden at Dakshineswar, where he intended to lead a spiritual life. He loved to argue and the Master often pointed him out as an example of barren argumentation. He was hypercritical of others and cherished an exaggerated notion of his own spiritual advancement. He was mischievous and often tried to upset the minds of the Master's young disciples, criticizing them for their happy and joyous life and asking them to devote their time to meditation. The Master teasingly compared Hāzrā to Jatilā and Kutilā, the two women who always created obstructions in Krishna's sport with the gopīs, and said that Hāzrā lived at Dakshineswar to "thicken the plot" by adding complications.

SOME NOTED MEN

Sri Ramakrishna also became acquainted with a number of people whose scholarship or wealth entitled them everywhere to respect. He had met, a few years before, Devendranāth Tāgore, famous all over Bengal for his wealth, scholarship, saintly character and social position. But the Master found him disappointing; for, whereas Sri Ramakrishna expected of a saint complete renunciation of the world, Devendranāth combined with his saintliness a life of enjoyment. Sri Ramakrishna met the great poet Michael Madhusūdan, who had embraced Christianity "for the sake of his stomach". To him the Master could not impart instruction, for the divine Mother "pressed his tongue". In addition he met Mahārājā Jatindramohan Tāgore, a titled aristocrat of Bengal; Kristodās Pāl, the editor, Social Reformer, and patriot; Iswar Vidyāsāgar, the noted philanthropist and

R—7

educator; Pundit Shashadhar, a great champion of Hindu ortho-
doxy ; Aswinīkumār Dutta, a Headmaster, moralist and leader
of Indian nationalism; and Bankim Chātterjī, a deputy magistrate, novelist and essayist, and one of the fashioners of modern
Bengali prose. Sri Ramakrishna was not the man to be dazzled
by outward show, glory or eloquence. A pundit without discrimination he regarded as a mere straw. He would search
people's hearts for the light of God; and if that was missing he
would have nothing to do with them.

KRISTODĀS PĀL

The Europeanized Kristodās Pāl did not approve of the
Master's emphasis on renunciation and said: "Sir, this cant of
renunciation has almost ruined the country. It is for this reason
that the Indians are a subject nation today. Doing good to
others, bringing education to the door of the ignorant and above
all, improving the material conditions of the country—these
should be our duty now. The cry of religion and renunciation
would, on the contrary, only weaken us. You should advise the
young men of Bengal to resort only to such acts as will uplift the
country." Sri Ramakrishna gave him a searching look and found
no divine light within. "You man of poor understanding!" Sri
Ramakrishna said sharply. "You dare to slight in these terms
renunciation and piety, which our scriptures describe as the
greatest of all virtues! After reading two pages of English you
think you have come to know the world! You appear to think
you are omniscient. Well, have you seen those tiny crabs that
are born in the Ganges just when the rains set in? In this big
universe you are even less significant than one of those small
creatures. How dare you talk of *helping* the world? The Lord
will look to that. You haven't the power in you to do it." After
a pause the Master continued : "Can you explain to me how you
can work for others? I know what you mean by helping them.

To feed a number of persons, to treat them when they are sick, to construct a road or dig a well—isn't that all ? These are good deeds, no doubt, but how trifling in comparison with the vastness of the universe ! How far can a man advance in this line ? How many people can you save from famine ? Malaria has ruined a whole province; what could you do to stop its onslaught ? God alone looks after the world. Let a man first realize Him. Let a man get the authority from God and be endowed with His power; then and then alone, may he think of doing good to others. A man should first be purged of all egotism. Then alone will the blissful Mother ask him to work for the world." Sri Ramakrishna mistrusted philanthropy that presumed to pose as charity. He warned people against it. He saw in most acts of philanthropy nothing but egotism, vanity, a desire for glory, a barren excitement to kill the boredom of life or an attempt to soothe a guilty conscience. True charity, he taught, is the result of love of God—service to man in a spirit of worship.

MONASTIC DISCIPLES

The disciples whom the Master trained for monastic life were the following :

Narendranāth Dutta (Swami Vivekananda)
Rakhālchandra Ghosh (Swami Brahmānanda)
Gopāl Sur (Swami Advaitānanda)
Bāburām Ghosh (Swami Premānanda)
Tāraknāth Ghoshāl (Swami Shivānanda)
Jōgīndranāth Choudhury (Swami Jogānanda)
S'ashībhūshan Chakravarty (Swami Ramakrishnānanda)
Saratchandra Chakravarty (Swami Sāradānanda)
Lātu (Swami Adbhutānanda)
Nitya Niranjan Sen (Swami Niranjanānanda)
Kāliprasād Chandra (Swami Abhedānanda)

Harināth Chattopādhyāya (Swami Turīāyānanda)
Sāradāprasanna (Swami Trigunatītānanda)
Gangādhar Ghatak (Swami Akhandānanda)
Subodh Ghosh (Swami Subodhānanda)
Hariprasanna Chātterjī (Swami Vijnānānanda)

LĀTU

The first of these young men to come to the Master was Lātu. Born of obscure parents, in Behar, he came to Calcutta in search of work and was engaged by Ramchandra Dutta as house-boy. Learning of the saintly Sri Ramakrishna, he visited the Master at Dakshineswar and was deeply touched by his cordiality. When he was about to leave, the Master asked him to take some money and return home in a boat or carriage. But Lātu declared he had a few pennies and jingled the coins in his pocket. Sri Ramakrishna later requested Ram to allow Lātu to stay with him permanently. Under Sri Ramakrishna's guidance Lātu made great progress in meditation and was blessed with ecstatic visions, but all the efforts of the Master to give him a smattering of education failed. Lātu was very fond of kīrtan and other devotional songs but remained all his life illiterate.

RĀKHĀL

Even before Rākhāl's coming to Dakshineswar, the Master had had visions of him as his spiritual son and as a playmate of Krishna at Vrindāvan. Rākhāl was born of wealthy parents. During his childhood he developed wonderful spiritual traits and used to play at worshipping gods and goddesses. In his teens he was married to a sister of Manomohan Mitra, from whom he first heard of the Master. His father objected to his association with Sri Ramakrishna but afterwards was reassured to find that many celebrated people were visitors at Dakshineswar. The relationship between the Master and this beloved disciple was that of mother and child. · Sri Ramakrishna allowed Rākhāl many liberties denied to others. But he would not hesitate to chastise the boy for improper actions. At one time Rākhāl felt a childlike jealousy because he found that other boys were receiving the Master's affection. He soon got over it and realized his guru as the guru of the whole universe. The Master was worried to hear of his marriage, but was relieved to find that his wife was a spiritual soul who would not be a hindrance to his progress.

THE ELDER GOPĀL

Gopāl Sur of Sinthi came to Dakshineswar at a rather advanced age and was called the elder Gopāl. He had lost his wife and the Master assuaged his grief. Soon he renounced the world and devoted himself fully to meditation and prayer. Some years later Gopāl gave the Master the ochre cloths with which the latter initiated several of his disciples into monastic life.

CHAPTER VI

NARENDRANĀTH AND OTHER DISCIPLES

To spread his message to the four corners of the earth Sri Ramakrishna needed a strong instrument. With his frail body and delicate limbs he could not make great journeys across wide spaces. And such an instrument was found in Narendranāth Dutta, his beloved Naren, later known to the world as Swami Vivekananda. Even before meeting Narendranāth, the Master had seen him in a vision as a sage, immersed in the meditation of the Absolute, who at Sri Ramakrishna's request had agreed to take human birth to assist him in his work.

Narendra was born in Calcutta on January 12, 1863, of an aristocratic kāyastha family. His mother was steeped in the great Hindu epics, and his father, a distinguished attorney of the Calcutta High Court, was an agnostic about religion, a friend of the poor, and a mocker at social conventions. Even in his boyhood and youth Narendra possessed great physical courage and presence of mind, a vivid imagination, deep power of thought, keen intelligence, an extraordinary memory, a love of truth, a passion for purity, a spirit of independence and a tender heart. An expert musician, he also acquired proficiency in physics, astronomy, mathematics, philosophy, history and literature. He grew up into an extremely handsome young man. Even as a child he practised meditation and showed great power of concentration. Though free and passionate in word and action, he took the vow of austere religious chastity and never allowed the fire of purity to be extinguished by the slightest defilement of body or soul.

As he read in college the rationalistic Western philosophers of the nineteenth century, his boyhood faith in God and religion was unsettled. He would not accept religion on mere faith ; he wanted demonstration of God. But very soon his passionate nature discovered that mere universal reason was old and bloodless. His emotional nature, dissatisfied with a mere abstraction required a concrete support to help him in the hours of temptation. He wanted an external power, a guru, who by embodying perfection in the flesh would still the commotion of his soul. Attracted by the magnetic personality of Keshab, he joined the Brāhmo Samāj and became a singer in its choir. But in the Samāj he did not find the guru who could say that he had seen God.

In a state of mental conflict and torture of soul, Narendra came to Sri Ramakrishna at Dakshineswar. He was then eighteen years of age and had been in college two years. He entered the Master's room accompanied by some light hearted friends. At Sri Ramakrishna's request he sang a few songs, pouring his whole soul into them and the Master went into samādhi. A few minutes later Sri Ramakrishna suddenly left his seat, took Narendra by the hand and led him to the screened verandah north of his room. They were alone. Addressing Narendra most tenderly, as if he were a friend of long acquaintance, the Master said: "Ah! You have come very late. Why have you been so unkind as to make me wait all these days ? My ears are tired of hearing the futile words of worldly men. Oh, how I have longed to pour my spirit into the heart of someone fitted to receive my message!" He talked thus, sobbing all the time. Then, standing before Narendra with folded hands, he addressed him as Nārāyana, born on earth to remove the misery of humanity. Grasping Narendra's hand, he asked him to come again, alone, and very soon. Narendra was startled. "What is this I have come to see?" he said to himself: "He must be stark mad. Why, I am the son of Viswanāth Dutta. How dare he speak this way to me?"

When they returned to the room and Narendra heard the Master speaking to others, he was surprised to find in his words an inner logic, a striking sincerity and a convincing proof of his spiritual nature. In answer to Narendra's question, "Sir, have you seen God?" the Master said: "Yes, I have seen God. I have seen Him more tangibly than I see you. I have talked to Him more intimately than I am talking to you." Continuing, the Master said: "But, my child, who wants to see God? People shed jugs of tears for money, wife and children. But if they would weep for God for only one day they would surely see Him." Narendra was amazed. These words he could not doubt. This was the first time he had ever heard a man saying that he had seen God. But he could not reconcile these words of the Master with the scene that had taken place on the verandah only a few minutes before. He concluded that Sri Ramakrishna was a monomaniac and returned home rather puzzled in mind.

During his second visit, about a month later, suddenly, at the touch of the Master, Narendra felt overwhelmed and saw the walls of the room and everything around him whirling and vanishing. "What are you doing to me?" he cried in terror. "I have my father and mother at home." He saw his own ego and the whole universe almost swallowed in a nameless void. With a laugh the Master easily restored him. Narendra thought he might have been hypnotized, but he could not understand how a monomaniac could cast a spell over the mind of a strong person like himself. He returned home more confused than ever, resolved to be henceforth on his guard before this strange man.

But during his third visit Narendra fared no better. This time, at the Master's touch, he lost consciousness entirely. While he was still in that state, Sri Ramakrishna questioned him concerning his spiritual antecedents and whereabouts, his mission in this world and the duration of his mortal life. The answers confirmed what the Master himself had known and inferred. Among other things, he came to know that Narendra was a sage who had already attained perfection and that the day he learnt his real nature he would give up his body in yoga, by an act of will.

A few more meetings completely removed from Narendra's mind the last traces of the notion that Sri Ramakrishna might be a monomaniac or wily hypnotist. His integrity, purity, renunciation, and unselfishness were beyond question. But Narendra could not accept a man, an imperfect mortal, as his guru. As a member of the Brāhmo Samāj, he could not believe that a human intermediary was necessary between man and God. Moreover, he openly laughed at Sri Ramakrishna's visions as hallucinations. Yet in the secret chamber of his heart he bore a great love for the Master.

Sri Ramakrishna was grateful to the divine Mother for sending him one who doubted his own realizations. Often he asked Narendra to test him as the money-changers test their coins. He laughed at Narendra's biting criticism of his spiritual experiences and samādhi. When at times Narendra's sharp words distressed him, the divine Mother Herself would console him, saying: "Why do you listen to him? In a few days he will believe your every word." He could hardly bear Narendra's absences. Often he would weep bitterly for the sight of him. Sometimes Narendra would find the Master's love embarrassing; and one day he sharply scolded him, warning him that such infatuation would soon draw him down to the level of its object. The Master was distressed and prayed to the divine Mother. Then he said to Narendra: "You rogue, I won't listen to you any more. Mother says that I love you because I see God in you and the day I no longer see God in you I shall not be able to bear even the sight of you."

The Master wanted to train Narendra in the teachings of the non-dualistic Vedānta philosophy. But Narendra, because of his Brāhmo upbringing, considered it wholly blasphemous to look on man as one with his creator. One day at the temple garden he laughingly said to a friend: "How silly! This jug is God! This cup is God! Whatever we see is God! And we too are God! Nothing could be more absurd." Sri Ramakrishna came out of his room and gently touched him. Spellbound, he immediately perceived that everything in the world was indeed God. A new universe opened around him. Returning home in a dazed state, he found there too that the food, the plate, the eater himself, the people around him, were all God. When he walked in the street, he saw that the cabs, the horses, the streams of people, the buildings, were all Brahman. He could hardly go about his day's business. His parents became anxious about him and thought him ill. And when the intensity of the experience abated a little, he saw the world as a dream. Walking in the public square, he would strike his head against the iron-railings to know whether they were real. It took him a number of days to recover his normal self. He had a foretaste of the great experiences yet to come and realized that the words of the Vedānta were true.

At the beginning of 1884 Narendra's father suddenly died of heart-failure, leaving the family in a state of utmost poverty. There were six or seven mouths to feed at home. Creditors were knocking at the door. Relatives who had accepted his father's unstinted kindness now became enemies, some even bringing suit to deprive Narendra of his ancestral home. Actually starving and barefoot, Narendra searched for a job, but without success. He began to doubt whether anywhere in the world there was such a thing as unselfish sympathy. Two rich women made evil proposals to him and promised to put an end to his distress, but he refused them with contempt.

Narendra began to talk of his doubt of the very existence of God. His friends thought he had become an atheist and piously circulated gossip adducing unmentionable motives for his unbelief. His moral character was maligned. Even some of the Master's disciples partly believed the gossip and Narendra told these to their faces that only a coward believed in God through fear of suffering or hell. But he was distressed to think that Sri Ramakrishna, too, might believe these false reports. His pride revolted. He said to himself: " What does it matter? If a man's good name rests on such slender foundations, I don't care." But later on he was amazed to learn that the Master had never lost faith in him. To a disciple who complained about Narendra's degradation, Sri Ramakrishna replied : " Hush, you fool! The Mother has told me it can never be so. I won't look at you if you speak that way again."

The moment came when Narendra's distress reached its climax. He had gone the whole day without food. As he was returning home in the evening he could hardly lift his tired limbs. He sat down in front of a house in sheer exhaustion, too weak even to think. His mind began to wander. Then, suddenly, a divine power lifted the veil over his soul. He found the solution of the problem of the coexistence of divine justice and misery, the presence of suffering in the creation of a blissful Providence. He felt bodily refreshed, his soul was bathed in peace and he slept serenely.

Narendra now realized that he had a spiritual mission to fulfil. He resolved to renounce the world, as his grandfather had renounced it and he came to Sri Ramakrishna for his blessing. But even before he had opened his mouth, the Master knew what was in his mind and wept bitterly at the thought of separation. "I know you cannot lead a worldly life," he said, " but for my sake live in the world as long as I live."

One day, soon after, Narendra requested Sri Ramakrishna to pray to the divine Mother to remove his poverty. Sri Ramakrishna bade him pray to Her himself for She would certainly listen to his prayer. Narendra entered the shrine of Kāli. As he stood before the image of the Mother, he beheld Her as a living Goddess, ready to give wisdom and liberation. Unable to ask Her for petty worldly things, he prayed only for knowledge and renunciation, love and liberation. The Master rebuked him for his failure to ask the divine Mother to remove his poverty and sent him back to the temple. But Narendra, standing in Her presence, again forgot the purpose of his coming. Thrice he went to the temple at the bidding of the Master and thrice he returned, having forgotten in Her presence why he had come. He was wondering about it when it suddenly flashed in his mind that this was all the work of Sri Ramakrishna; so now he asked the Master himself to remove his poverty and was assured that his family would not lack simple food and clothing.

This was a very rich and significant experience for Narendra. It taught him that S'akti, the divine Power, cannot be ignored in the world and that in the relative plane the need of worshipping a personal God is imperative. Sri Ramakrishna was overjoyed with the conversion. The next day, sitting almost on Narendra's lap, he said to a devotee, pointing first to himself, then to Narendra: " I see I am this and again that. Really I feel no difference. A stick floating in the Ganges seems to divide the water; but in reality the water is one. Do you see my point? Well, whatever is, is the Mother—isn't that so?" In later years Narendra would say: " Sri Ramakrishna was the only person who, from the time he met me, believed in me uniformly throughout. Even my mother and brothers did not. It was his unwavering trust and love for me that bound me to him for ever.

He alone knew how to love.   Worldly people only make a show
of love for selfish ends. "

TĀRAK

Others, destined to be monastic disciples of Sri Ramakrishna
came to Dakshineswar. Tāraknāth Ghoshāl had felt from his
boyhood the noble desire to realize God. Keshab and the
Brāhmo Samāj had attracted him but proved inadequate. In
1882 he first met the Master at Ramachandra's house and was
astonished to hear him talk about samādhi, a subject which
always fascinated his mind. And that evening he actually saw a
manifestation of that superconscious state in the Master. Tārak
became a frequent visitor at Dakshineswar and received the
Master's grace in abundance. The young boy often felt ecstatic
fervour in meditation. He also wept profusely while meditating
on God. Sri Ramakrishna said to him : " God favours those
who can weep for Him. Tears shed for God wash away the sins
of former births. "

BĀBURĀM

Bāburām Ghosh came to Dakshineswar accompanied by
Rākhāl, his classmate. The Master, as was often his custom,
examined the boy's physiognomy and was satisfied about his
latent spirituality. At the age of eight Bāburām had thought of
leading a life of renunciation in the company of a monk, in a
hut shut out from the public view by a thick wall of trees. The
very sight of the Panchavatī awakened in his heart that dream of
boyhood. Bāburām was tender in body and soul. The Master
used to say that he was pure to his very bones. One day Hāzrā
in his usual mischievous fashion advised Bāburām and some of
the other young boys to ask Sri Ramakrishna for some spiritual
powers and not waste their life in mere gaiety and merriment.
The Master, scenting mischief, called Bāburām to his side and

said: " What can you ask of me? Isn't everything that I have, already yours? Yes, everything I have earned in the shape of realizations is for the sake of you all. So get rid of the idea of begging which alienates by creating a distance. Rather realize your kinship with me and gain the key to all the treasures. "

NIRANJAN

Nitya Niranjan Ghosh was a disciple of heroic type. He came to the Master when he was eighteen years old. He was a medium for a group of spiritualists. During his first visit the Master said to him : " My boy, if you think always of ghosts you will become a ghost and if you think of God you will become God. Now, which do you prefer?" Niranjan severed all connections with the spiritualists. During his second visit the Master embraced him and said warmly: " Niranjan, my boy, the days are flitting away. When will you realize God ? This life will be in vain if you do not realize Him. When will you devote your mind wholly to God ? " Niranjan was surprised to see the Master's great anxiety for his spiritual welfare. He was a young man endowed with unusual spiritual parts. He felt disdain for worldly pleasures and was totally guileless like a child. But he had a violent temper. One day, as he was coming in a country boat to Dakshineswar, some of his fellow-passengers began to speak ill of the Master. Finding his protest futile, Niranjan began to rock the boat, threatening to sink it in mid stream. That silenced the offenders. When he reported the incident to the Master, he was rebuked for his inability to curb his anger.

JOGINDRA

Jogindranath, on the other hand, was gentle to a fault. One day, under circumstances very like those that had evoked Niranjan's anger, he curbed his temper and held his peace instead of threatening Sri Ramakrishna's abusers. The Master, learning of his conduct, scolded him roundly. Thus to each, the fault of the other was recommended as a virtue. The guru was striving to develop, in the first instane, composure and in the second, mettle. The secret of his training was to build up, by a tactful recognition of the requirements of each given case, the character of the devotee.

Jogindranath came of an aristocratic brāhmin family of Dakshineswar. His father and relatives shared the popular mistrust of Sri Ramakrishna's sanity. At a very early age the boy developed religious tendencies, spending two or three hours daily in meditation and his meeting with Sri Ramakrishna deepened his desire for the realization of God. He had a perfect horror of marriage. But at the earnest request of his mother he had had to yield and he now believed that his spiritual future was doomed. So he kept himself away from the Master.

Sri Ramakrishna employed a ruse to bring Jogindra to him. As soon as the disciple entered the room, the Master rushed forward to meet the young man. Catching hold of the disciple's hand, he said: "What if you have married? Haven't I too married? What is there to be afraid of in that? Touching his own chest he said: "If this [meaning himself] is propitious, then even a hundred thousand marriages cannot injure you. If you desire to lead a householder's life, then bring your wife here one day and I shall see that she becomes a real companion in your spiritual progress. But if you want to lead a monastic life, then I shall eat up your attachment to the world." Jogin was dumbfounded at these words. He received new strength and his spirit of renunciation was re-established.

S'ASHĪ AND S'ARAT

S'ashī and S'arat were two cousins who came from a pious brāhmin family of Calcutta. At an early age they had joined the

Brāhmo Samāj and had come under the influence of Keshab Sen. The Master said to them at their first meeting: "If bricks and tiles are burnt after the trade-mark has been stamped on them, they retain the mark for ever. Similarly, man should be stamped with God before entering the world. Then he will not become attached to worldliness." Fully aware of the future course of their life, he asked them not to marry. The Master asked S'ashi whether he believed in God with form or in God without form. S'ashi replied that he was not even sure about the existence of God; so he could not speak one way or the other. This frank answer very much pleased the Master.

S'arat's soul longed for the all-embracing realization of the Godhead. When the Master inquired whether there was any particular form of God he wished to see, the boy replied that he would like to see God in all the living beings of the world. "But" the Master demurred, "that is the last word in realization. One cannot have it at the very outset." S'arat stated calmly: "I won't be satisfied with anything short of that. I shall trudge on along the path till I attain that blessed state." Sri Ramakrishna was very much pleased.

HARINĀTH

Harināth had led the austere life of a brahmachāri even from his early boyhood—bathing in the Ganges every day, cooking his own meals, waking before sunrise, and reciting the *Gita* from memory before leaving bed. He found in the Master the embodiment of the Vedānta scriptures. Aspiring to be a follower of the ascetic S'ankara, he cherished a great hatred for women. One day he said to the Master that he could not allow even small girls to come near him. The Master scolded him and said: "You are talking like a fool. Why should you hate women? They are the manifestations of the divine Mother. Regard them as your own mother and you will never feel their evil influence. The more you hate them, the more you will fall into their snares." Hari said later that these words completely changed his attitude toward women.

The Master knew Hari's passion for Vedānta. But he did not wish any of his disciples to become a dry ascetic or a mere bookworm. So he asked Hari to practise Vedānta in life by giving up the unreal and following the real. " But it is not so easy ", Sri Ramakrishna said. " to realize the illusoriness of the world. Study alone does not help one very much. The grace of God is required. Mere personal effort is futile. A man is a tiny creature after all, with very limited powers. But he can achieve the impossible if he prays to God for His grace." Whereupon the Master sang a song in praise of grace. Hari was profoundly moved and shed tears. Later in life Hari achieved a wonderful synthesis of the ideals of the personal God and the impersonal truth.

GANGĀDHAR

Gangādhar, Harināth's friend, also led the life of a strict brahmachārī, eating vegetarian food cooked by his own hands and devoting himself to the study of the scriptures. He met the Master in 1884 and soon became a member of his inner circle. The Master praised his ascetic habit and attributed it to the spiritual disciplines of his past life. Gangādhar became a close companion of Narendra.

HARIPRĀSANNA

Hariprasanna, a college student, visited the Master in the company of his friends Sashī and Sarat. Sri Ramakrishna showed him great favour by initiating him into spiritual life. As long as he lived, Hariprasanna remembered and observed the following drastic advice of the Master : "Even if a woman is pure
R—8

as gold and rolls on the ground for love of God it is dangerous for a monk ever to look at her."

KĀLĪ

Kālīprasād visited the Master toward the end of 1883. Given to the practice of meditation and the study of the scriptures, Kālī was particularly interested in yoga. Feeling the need of a guru in spiritual life, he came to the Master and was accepted as a disciple. The young boy possessed a rational mind and often felt sceptical about the personal God. The Master said to him: "Your doubts will soon disappear. Others, too, have passed through such a state of mind. Look at Naren. He now weeps at the names of Rādhā and Krishna." Kālī began to see visions of gods and goddesses. Very soon these disappeared and in meditation he experienced vastness, infinity and the other attributes of the impersonal Brahman.

SUBODH

Subodh visited the Master in 1885. At the very first meeting Sri Ramakrishna said to him: "You will succeed. Mother says so. Those whom She sends here will certainly attain spirituality." During the second meeting the Master wrote something cn Subodh's tongue, stroked his body from the navel to the throat and said, "Awake, Mother! Awake." He asked the boy to meditate. At once Subodh's latent spirituality was awakened. He felt a current rushing along the spinal column to the brain. Joy filled his soul.

SĀRADĀ

Another young man, Sāradāprasanna completes the small band of the Master's disciples later to embrace the life of the wandering monk. With the exception of the elder Gopāl, all of them were in their teens or slightly over. They came from middle-class Bengali families, and most of them were students in school or college. Their parents and relatives had envisaged for them bright worldly careers. They came to Sri Ramakrishna with pure bodies, vigorous minds and uncontaminated souls. All were born with unusual spiritual attributes. Sri Ramakrishna accepted them, even at first sight, as his children, relatives friends and companions. His magic touch unfolded them. And later each according to his measure reflected the life of the Master, becoming a torch-bearer of his message across land and sea.

WOMAN DEVOTEES

With his woman devotees Sri Ramakrishna established a very sweet relationship. He himself embodied the tender traits of a woman; he had dwelt on the highest plane of truth, where there is not even the slightest trace of sex; and his innate purity evoked only the noblest emotion in men and women alike. His woman devotees often said: "We seldom looked on Sri Ramakrishna as a member of the male sex. We regarded him as one of us. We never felt any constraint before him. He was our best confidant." They loved him as their child, their friend, and their teacher. In spiritual discipline he advised them to renounce lust and greed and especially warned them not to fall into the snares of men.

GOPAL MA

Unsurpassed among the woman devotees of the Master in the richness of her devotion and spiritual experiences was Aghoremani Devi, an orthodox brahmin woman. Widowed at an early age, she had dedicated herself completely to spiritual pursuits. Gopala, the baby Krishna, was her ideal Deity, whom she worshipped following the vātsalya attitude of the Vaishnava religion, regarding Him as her own child. Through

Him she satisfied her unassuaged maternal love, cooking for Him feeding Him, bathing Him and putting Him to bed. This sweet intimacy with Gopāla won her the sobriquet of Gopāl Mā, or Gopāla's Mother. For forty years she had lived on the bank of the Ganges in a small, bare room, her only companions being a threadbare copy of the *Rāmāyana* and a bag containing her rosary. At the age of sixty, in 1884, she visited Sri Ramakrishna at Dakshineswar. During the second visit, as soon as the Master saw her, he said : "Oh, you have come! Give me something to eat." With great hesitation she gave him some ordinary sweets that she had purchased for him on the way. The Master ate them with relish and asked her to bring him simple curries or sweets prepared by her own hands. Gopāl Mā thought him a queer kind of monk, for, instead of talking of God, he always asked for food. She did not want to visit him again, but an irresistible attraction brought her back to the temple garden. She carried with her some simple curries that she had cooked herself.

One early morning at three o'clock, about a year later, Gopāl Mā was about to finish her daily devotions, when she was startled to find Sri Ramakrishna sitting on her left, with his right hand clenched, like the hand of the image of Gopāla. She was amazed and caught hold of the hand, whereupon the figure vanished and in its place appeared the real Gopāla, her ideal Deity. She cried aloud with joy. Gopāla begged her for butter. She pleaded her poverty and gave Him some dry coconut candies. Gopāla sat on her lap, snatched away her rosary, jumped on her shoulders and moved all about the room. As soon as the day broke she hastened to Dakshineswar like an insane woman. Of course Gopāla accompanied her, resting His head on her shoulder. She clearly saw His tiny ruddy feet hanging over her breast. She entered Sri Ramakrishna's room. The Master had fallen, into samādhi. Like a child, he sat on her lap and she began to feed him with butter, cream, and other delicacies. After some time he regained consciousness and returned to his bed. But the mind of Gopala's Mother was still roaming in another plane. She was steeped in bliss. She saw Gopāla frequently entering the Master's body and again coming out of it. When she returned to her hut, still in a dazed condition, Gopāla accompanied her.

She spent about two months in uninterrupted communion with God, the Baby Gopāla never leaving her for a moment. Then the intensity of her vision was lessened; had it not been, her body would have perished. The Master spoke highly of her exalted spiritual condition and said that such vision of God was a rare thing for ordinary mortals. The fun-loving Master one day confronted the critical Narendranāth with this simple-minded woman. No two could have presented a more striking contrast. The Master knew of Narendra's lofty contempt for all visions and he asked the old lady to narrate her experiences to Narendra. With great hesitation she told him her story. Now and then she interrupted her maternal chatter to ask Narendra : " My son, I am a poor ignorant woman. I don't understand anything. You are so learned. Now tell me if these visions of Gopāla are true." As Narendra listened to the story he was profoundly moved. He said, " Yes, mother, they are quite true." Behind his cynicsm Narendra, too, possessed a heart full of love and tenderness.

THE MARCH OF EVENTS

In 1881 Hriday was dismissed from service in the Kāli temple, for an act of indiscretion and was ordered by the authorities never again to enter the garden. In a way the hand of the divine Mother may be seen even in this. Having taken care of Sri Ramakrishna during the stormy days of his spiritual discipline, Hriday had come naturally to consider himself the sole guardian of his uncle. None could approach the Master without

his knowledge. And he would be extremely jealous if Sri Ramakrishna paid attention to anyone else. Hriday's removal made it
possible for the real devotees of the Master to approach him
freely and live with him in the temple garden.

During the week-ends the householders, enjoying a respite
from their office duties, visited the Master. The meetings on
Sunday afternoons were of the nature of little festivals. Refreshments were often served. Professional musicians now and then
sang devotional songs. The Master and the devotees sang and
danced, Sri Ramakrishna frequently going into ecstatic moods.
The happy memory of such a Sunday would linger long in the
minds of the devotees. Those whom the Master wanted for
special instruction he would ask to visit him on Tuesdays and
Saturdays. These days were particularly auspicious for the
worship of Kāli.

The young disciples destined to be monks, Sri Ramakrishna
invited on week-days, when the householders were not present.
The training of the householders and of the future monks had to
proceed along entirely different lines. Since M. generally visited
the Master on week-ends, the *Gospel of Sri Ramakrishna* does
not contain much mention of the future monastic disciples.

Finally, there was a handful of fortunate disciples, householders as well as youngsters, who were privileged to spend nights
with the Master in his room. They would see him get up early in
the morning and walk up and down the room, singing in his sweet
voice and tenderly communing with the Mother.

INJURY TO THE MASTER'S ARM

One day, in January 1884, the Master was going toward
the pine-grove when he went into a trance. He was alone.
There was no one to support him or guide his footsteps. He fell

to the ground and dislocated a bone in his left arm. This accident had a significant influence on his mind, the natural inclination of which was to soar above the consciousness of the body. The acute pain in the arm forced his mind to dwell on the body and on the world outside. But he saw even in this a divine purpose; for with his mind compelled to dwell on the physical plane, he realized more than ever that he was an instrument in the hand of the divine Mother, who had a mission to fulfil through his human body and mind. He also distinctly found that in the phenomenal world God manifests Himself, in an inscrutable way, through diverse human beings, both good and evil. Thus he would speak of God in the guise of the wicked, God in the guise of the pious, God in the guise of the hypocrite, God in the guise of the lewd. He began to take a special delight in watching the divine play in the relative world. Sometimes the sweet human relationship with God would appear to him more appealing than the all-effacing knowledge of Brahman. Many a time he would pray: " Mother, don't make me unconscious through the knowledge of Brahman. Don't give me Brahmajnāna, Mother. Am I not Your child, and naturally timid? I must have my Mother. A million salutations to the knowledge of Brahman! Give it to those who want it." Again he prayed: " O Mother, let me remain in contact with men! Don't make me a dried-up ascetic. I want to enjoy Your sport in the world." He was able to taste this very rich divine experience and enjoy the love of God and the company of His devotees because his mind, on account of the injury to his arm, was forced to. come down to the consciousness of the body. Again, he would make fun of people who proclaimed him as a divine Incarnation, by pointing to his broken arm. He would say, " Have you ever heard of God breaking His arm? " It took the arm about five months to heal.

CHAPTER VII

ILLNESS AND MAHĀSAMĀDHI

IN April 1885 the Master's throat became inflamed. Prolonged conversation or absorption in samādhi, making the blood flow into the throat, would aggravate the pain. Yet when the annual Vaishnava festival was celebrated at Pānihāti, Sri Ramakrishna attended it against the doctor's advice. With a group of disciples he spent himself in music, dance, and ecstasy. The illness took a turn for the worse and was diagnosed as "clergyman's sore throat." The patient was cautioned against conversation and ecstasies. Though he followed the physician's directions regarding medicine and diet, he could neither control his trances nor withhold from seekers the solace of his advice. Sometimes, like a sulky child, he would complain to the Mother about the crowds, who gave him no rest day or night. He was overheard to say to Her: "Why do You bring here all these worthless people, who are like milk diluted with five times its own quantity of water? My eyes are almost destroyed with blowing the fire to dry up the water. My health is gone. It is beyond my strength. Do it Yourself, if You want it done. This (*pointing to his own body*) is but a perforated drum and if you go on beating it day in and day out, how long will it last?"

But his large heart never turned anyone away. He said, "Let me be condemned to be born over and over again, even in the form of a dog, if I can be of help to a single soul." And he bore the pain, singing cheerfully, "Let the body be preoccupied with illness, but, O mind, dwell for ever in God's bliss!"

One night he had a hemorrhage of the throat. The doctor now diagnosed the illness as cancer. Narendra was the first to break this heart-rending news to the disciples. Within three days the Master was removed to Calcutta for better treatment. At Balarām's house he remained a week until a suitable place could be found at S'yāmpukur, in the northern section of Calcutta. During this week he dedicated himself practically without respite to the instruction of those beloved devotees who had been unable to visit him oftener at Dakshineswar. Discourses incessantly flowed from his tongue and he often went into samādhi. Dr. Mahendralāl Sarkār, the celebrated homeopath of Calcutta, was invited to undertake his treatment.

S'YĀMPUKUR

In the beginning of September 1885, Sri Ramakrishna was moved to Śyāmpukur. Here Narendra organized the young disciples to attend the Master day and night. At first they concealed the Master's illness from their guardians; but when it became more serious they remained with him almost constantly, sweeping aside the objections of their relatives and devoting themselves whole-heartedly to the nursing of their beloved guru. These young men, under the watchful eyes of the Master and the leadership of Narendra, became the *antaranga bhaktas*, the devotees of Sri Ramakrishna's inner circle. They were privileged to witness many manifestations of the Master's divine powers. Narendra received instructions regarding the propagation of his message after his death.

The Holy Mother—so Sāradā Devī had come to be affectionately known by Sri Ramakrishna's devotees—was brought from Dakshineswar to look after the general cooking and to prepare the special diet of the patient. The dwelling space being extremely limited, she had to adapt herself to cramped conditions. At three o'clock in the morning she would finish her bath in the Ganges and then enter a small covered place on the roof, where she spent the whole day cooking and praying. After eleven at night, when the visitors went away, she would come down to her small bedroom on the first floor to enjoy a few hours' sleep. Thus she spent three months, working hard, sleeping little and praying constantly for the Master's recovery.

At S'yāmpukur the devotees led an intense life. Their attendance on the Master was in itself a form of spiritual discipline. His mind was constantly soaring to an exalted plane of consciousness. Now and then they would catch the contagion of his spiritual fervour. They sought to divine the meaning of this illness of the Master, whom most of them had accepted as an Incarnation of God. One group, headed by Girish with his robust optimism and great power of imagination, believed that the illness was a mere pretext to serve a deeper purpose. The Master had willed his illness in order to bring the devotees together and promote solidarity among them. As soon as this purpose was served, he would himself get rid of the disease. A second group thought that the divine Mother, in whose hand the Master was an instrument, had brought about this illness to serve Her own mysterious ends. But the young rationalists, led by Narendra, refused to ascribe a supernatural cause to a natural phenomenon. They believed that the Master's body, a material thing, was subject, like all other material things, to physical laws. Growth, development, decay and death were laws of nature to which the Master's body could not but respond. But though holding differing views, they all believed that it was to him alone that they must look for the attainment of their spiritual goal.

In spite of the physician's efforts and the prayers and nursing of the devotees, the illness rapidly progressed. The pain sometimes appeared to be unbearable. The Master lived only on liquid food and his frail body was becoming a mere skeleton. Yet his face always radiated joy and he continued to welcome the visitors pouring in to receive his blessing. When certain zealous devotees tried to keep the visitors away, they were told by Girish, "You cannot succeed in it; he has been born for this very purpose—to sacrifice himself for the redemption of others."

The more the body was devastated by illness, the more it became the habitation of the divine Spirit. Through its transparency the gods and goddesses began to shine with ever increasing luminosity. On the day of the Kālī Pujā the devotees clearly saw in him the manifestation of the divine Mother.

It was noticed at this time that some of the devotees were making an unbridled display of their emotions. A number of them, particularly among the householders, began to cultivate, though at first unconsciously, the art of shedding tears, shaking the body, contorting the face and going into trances, attempting thereby to imitate the Master. They began openly to declare Sri Ramakrishna a divine Incarnation and to regard themselves as his chosen people, who could neglect religious disciplines with impunity. Narendra's penetrating eye soon sized up the situation. He found out that some of these external manifestations were being carefully practised at home, while some were the outcome of malnutrition, mental weakness or nervous debility. He mercilessly exposed the devotees who were pretending to have visions and asked all to develop a healthy religious spirit. Narendra sang inspiring songs for the younger devotees, read with them the *Imitation of Christ* and the *Gita* and held before them the positive ideals of spirituality.

LAST DAYS AT COSSIPORE

When Sri Ramakrishna's illness showed signs of aggravation, the devotees, following the advice of Dr. Sarkār, rented a spacious garden house at Cossipore, in the northern suburbs of Calcutta. The Master was removed to this place on December 11, 1885.

It was at Cossipore that the curtain fell on the varied activities of the Master's life on the physical plane. His soul lingered in the body eight months more. It was the period of his great passion, a constant crucifixion of the body and the triumphant revelation of the Soul. Here one sees the humanity and divinity of the Master passing and repassing across a thin border line. Every minute of those eight months was suffused with touching tenderness of heart and breath-taking elevation of spirit. Every word he uttered was full of pathos and sublimity.

It took the group only a few days to become adjusted to the new environment. The Holy Mother, assisted by Sri Ramakrishna's niece, Lakshmī Devī and a few woman devotees, took charge of cooking for the Master and his attendants. Surendra willingly bore the major portion of the expenses, other householders contributing according to their means. Twelve disciples were constant attendants of the Master : Narendra, Rākhāl, Bāburām, Niranjan, Jogin, Lātu, Tārak, the elder Gopāl, Kālī, Sashī, Sarat, and the younger Gopāl. Sāradā, Harish, Hari and Gangādhar visited the Master from time to time and practised sādhanā at home. Narendra, preparing for his law examination, brought his books to the garden house in order to continue his studies during the infrequent spare moments. He encouraged his brother disciples to intensify their meditation, scriptural studies and other spiritual disciplines. They all forgot their relatives and their worldly duties.

Among the attendants Sashī was the embodiment of service. He did not practise meditation, japa or any of the other disciplines followed by his brother devotees. He was convinced that service to the guru was the only religion for him. He forgot food and rest and was ever ready at the Master's bedside.

Pandit Shashadhar one day suggested to the Master that the latter could remove the illness by concentrating his mind on the throat, the scriptures having declared that yogīs had power to cure themselves in that way. The Master rebuked the pandit. "For a scholar like you to make such a proposal !" he said. "How can I withdraw the mind from the lotus feet of God and turn it to this worthless cage of flesh and blood ?" "For our sake at least ", begged Narendra and the other disciples. "But," replied Sri Ramakrishna, " do you think I enjoy this suffering ? I wish to recover, but that depends on the Mother."

NARENDRA : "Then please pray to Her. She must listen to you."

MASTER : " But I cannot pray for my body."

NARENDRA ; " You must do it for our sake at least."

MASTER : " Very well, I shall try."

A few hours later the Master said to Narendra: "I said to Her : ' Mother, I cannot swallow food because of my pain. Make it possible for me to eat a little.' She pointed you all out to me and said : ' What ? You are eating enough through all these mouths. Isn't that so ?' I was ashamed and could not utter another word." This dashed all the hopes of the devotees for the Master's recovery.

" I shall make the whole thing public before I go," the Master had said some time before. On January 1, 1886, he felt better and came down to the garden for a little stroll. It was about three o'clock in the afternoon. Some thirty lay disciples were in the hall or sitting about under the trees. Sri Rama- krishna said to Girish, " Well, Girish, what have you seen in me, that you proclaim me before everybody as an Incarnation of God?" Girish was not the man to be taken by surprise. He knelt before the Master and said with folded hands, " What can an insigni- ficant person like myself say about the one whose glory even

sages like Vyāsa and Vālmīki could not adequately measure?"
The Master was profoundly moved. He said: "What more
shall I say? I bless you all. Be illumined!" He fell into a
spiritual mood. Hearing these words the devotees, one and all,
became overwhelmed with emotion. They rushed to him and
fell at his feet. He touched them all and each received an
appropriate benediction. Each of them, at the touch of the
Master, experienced ineffable bliss. Some laughed, some wept,
some sat down to meditate, some began to pray. Some saw light,
some had vision of their chosen ideals, and some felt within
their bodies the rush of spiritual power.

Narendra, consumed with a terrific fever for realization,
complained to the Master that all the others had attained peace
and that he alone was dissatisfied. The Master asked what he
wanted. Narendra begged for samādhi, so that he might altogether
forget the world for three or four days at a time. "You are a
fool", the Master rebuked him. "There is a state even higher
than that. Isn't it you who sing, 'All that exists art Thou?'
First of all settle your family affairs and then come to me. You
will experience a state even higher then samādhi."

The Master did not hide the fact that he wished to make
Narendra his spiritual heir. Narendra was to continue the work
after Sri Ramakrishna's passing. Sri Ramakrishna said to him:
"I leave these young men in your charge. See that they develop
their spirituality and do not return home." One day he asked
the boys, in preparation for a monastic life, to beg their food from
door to door without thought of caste. They hailed the Master's
order and went out with begging-bowls. A few days later he
gave the ochre cloth of the sannyāsī to each of them, including
Girish, who was now second to none in his spirit of renunciation.
Thus the Master himself laid the foundation of the future
Ramakrishna Order of monks.

Sri Ramakrishna was sinking day by day. His diet was reduced to minimum and he found it almost impossible to swallow. He whispered to M.: "I am bearing all this cheerfully, for otherwise you would be weeping. If you all say that it is better that the body should go rather than suffer this torture, I am willing." The next morning he said to his depressed disciples seated near the bed: "Do you know what I see? I see that God alone has become everything. Men and animals are only frameworks covered with skin and it is He who is moving through their heads and limbs. I see that it is God Himself who has become the block, the executioner and the victim for the sacrifice." He fainted with emotion. Regaining partial consciousness, he said: "Now I have no pain. I am very well." Looking at Latu he said: "There sits Latu resting his head on the palm of his hand. To me it is the Lord who is seated in that posture."

The words were tender and touching. Like a mother he caressed Narendra and Rākhāl, gently stroking their faces. He said in a half whisper to M.. "Had this body been allowed to last a little longer, many more souls would have been illumined." He paused a moment and then said: "But mother has ordained otherwise. She will take me away lest, finding me guileless and foolish, people should take advantage of me and persuade me to bestow on them the rare gifts of spirituality." A few minutes later he touched his chest and said: "Here are two beings. One is She and the other is Her devotee. It is the latter who broke his arm, and it is he again who is now ill. Do you understand me?" After a pause he added: "Alas! To whom shall I tell all this? Who will understand me?" "Pain," he consoled them again, "is unavoidable as long as there is a body. The Lord takes on the body for the sake of His devotees."

Yet one is not sure whether the Master's soul actually was tortured by this agonizing disease. At least during his moments of spiritual exaltation—which became almost constant during the closing days of his life on earth—he lost all consciousness of the body, of illness and suffering. One of his attendants[9] said later on: "While Sri Ramakrishna lay sick he never actually suffered pain. He would often say: 'O mind! Forget the body, forget the sickness and remain merged in Bliss' No, he did not really suffer. At times he would be in a state when the thrill of joy was clearly manifested in his body. Even when he could not speak he would let us know in some way that there was no suffering, and this fact was clearly evident to all who watched him. People who did not understand him thought that his suffering was very great. What spiritual joy he transmitted to us at that time! Could such a thing have been possible if he had been suffering physically? It was during this period that he taught us again these truths: 'Brahman is always unattached. The three gunas are in It, but It is unaffected by them, just as the wind carries odour yet remains odourless.' 'Brahman is infinite Being, infinite Wisdom, infinite Bliss. In It there exist no delusion, no misery, no disease, no death, no growth, no decay.' 'The transcendental Being and the being within are one and the same. There is one indivisible absolute Existence.''

The Holy Mother secretly went to a S'iva temple across the Ganges to intercede with the Deity for the Master's recovery. In a revelation she was told to prepare herself for the inevitable end.

One day when Narendra was on the ground floor, meditating, the Master was lying awake in his bed upstairs. In the depths of his meditation Narendra felt as though a lamp were burning at the back of his head. Suddenly he lost consciousness.

---

[9] Latu, later known as Swami Adbhutananda.

It was the yearned-for, all-effacing experience of nirvikalpa samādhi, when the embodied soul realizes its unity with the Absolute. After a very long time he regained partial consciousness but was unable to find his body. He could see only his head. "Where is my body?" he cried. The elder Gopāl entered the room and said, "Why, it is here, Naren!" But Narendra could not find it. Gopāl, frightened, ran upstairs to the Master. Sri Ramakrishna only said: "Let him stay that way for a time. He has worried me long enough."

After another long period Narendra regained full consciousness. Bathed in peace, he went to the Master, who said: "Now the Mother has shown you everything. But this revelation will remain under lock and key and I shall keep the key. When you have accomplished the Mother's work you will find the treasure again."

Some days later, Narendra being alone with the Master, Sri Ramakrishna looked at him and went into samādhi. Narendra felt the penetration of a subtle force and lost all outer consciousness. Regaining presently the normal mood, he found the Master weeping.

Sri Ramakrishna said to him: "Today I have given you my all and I am now only a poor fakir, possessing nothing. By this power you will do immense good in the world, and not until it is accomplished will you return." Henceforth the Master lived in the disciple.

Doubt, however, dies hard. After one or two days Narendra said to himself, "If in the midst of this racking physical pain he declares his Godhead, then only shall I accept him as an Incarnation of God." He was alone by the bedside of the Master. It was a passing thought, but the Master smiled. Gathering his remaining strength, he distinctly said, "He who was Rāma and
R—9

Krishna is now, in this body, Ramakrishna—but not in your Vedāntic sense." Narendra was stricken with shame.

MAHĀSAMĀDHI

Sunday, August 15, 1886. The Master's pulse became irregular. The devotees stood by the bedside. Toward dusk Sri Ramakrishna had difficulty in breathing. A short time afterwards he complained of hunger. A little liquid food was put into his mouth; some of it he swallowed and the rest ran over his chin. Two attendants began to fan him. All at once he went into samādhi of a rather unusual type. The body became stiff. Sashī burst into tears. But after midnight the Master revived. He was now very hungry and helped himself to a bowl of porridge. He said he was strong again. He sat up against five or six pillows, which were supported by the body of Sashī, who was fanning him. Narendra took his feet on his lap and began to rub them. Again and again the Master repeated to him, "Take care of these boys." Then he was asked to lie down. Three times in ringing tones he cried the name of Kāli, his life's Beloved and lay back. At two minutes past one, there was a low sound in his throat and he fell a little to one side. A thrill passed over his body. His hair stood on end. His eyes became fixed on the tip of his nose. His face was lighted with a smile. The final ecstasy began. It was mahāsamādhi, total absorption, from which his mind never returned. Narendra, unable to bear it, ran downstairs.

Dr. Sarkār arrived the following noon and pronounced that life had departed not more than half an hour before. At five o'clock the Master's body was brought downstairs, laid on a cot, dressed in ochre clothes, and decorated with sandal-paste and flowers. A procession was formed. The passers-by wept as the body was taken to the cremation ground at the Barānagore Ghāt on the Ganges.

While the devotees were returning to the garden house, carrying the urn with the sacred ashes, a calm resignation came to their souls and they cried, " Victory unto the Guru ! "

The Holy Mother was weeping in her room, not for her husband, but because she felt that Mother Kāli had left her. As she was about to put on the marks of a Hindu widow, in a moment of revelation she heard the words of faith, " I have only passed from one room to another."

CHAPTER VIII

AFTER THE PASSING AWAY

$\mathcal{S}$RI RAMAKRISHNA passed away on Sunday, August 15, 1886, plunging his devotees and disciples into a sea of grief. They were like men in a shipwreck. But a strong bond of love held them together and they found assurance and courage in each other's company. They could not enjoy the friendship of worldly people and would talk only of their Master. " Shall we not behold him again ?—" this was the one theme of their thought and the one dream of their sleep. Alone, they wept for him ; walking in the streets of Calcutta, they were engrossed in the thought of him. The Master had once said to M., "It becomes difficult for me to give up the body, when I realize that after my death you will wander about weeping for me." Some of them thought : "He is no longer in this world. How surprising that we still enjoy living! We could give up our bodies if we liked, but still we do not." Time and again Sri Ramakrishna had told them that God reveals Himself to His devotees if they yearn for Him and call on Him with whole-souled devotion. He had assured them that God listens to the prayer of a sincere heart.

The young unmarried disciples of the Master, who belonged to his inner circle, had attended on him day and night at the Cossipore garden house. After his passing away most of them returned to their families against their own wills. They had not yet formally renounced the world. For a short while they kept their family names. But Sri Ramakrishna had made them renounce the world mentally. He himself had initiated several of them into the monastic life, giving them the ochre cloths of sannyāsīs.

Two or three of the Master's attendants had no place to go. To them the large-hearted Surendra said: "Brothers, where will you go? Let us rent a house. You will live their and make it our Master's shrine; and we house-holders shall come there for consolation. How can we pass all our days and nights with our wives and children in the world? I used to spend a sum of money for the Master at Cossipore. I shall gladly give it now for your expenses." Accordingly he rented a house for them at Barānagore, in the suburbs of Calcutta. and this place became gradually transformed into a math or monastery.

For the first few months Surendra contributed thirty rupees a month. As the other members joined the monastery one by one, he doubled his contribution, which he later increased to a hundred rupees. The monthly rent for the house was eleven rupees. The cook received six rupees a month. The rest was spent for food.

The younger Gopāl brought the Master's bed and other articles of daily use from the garden house at Cossipore. The Brāhmin who had been cook at Cossipore was engaged for the new monastery. The first permanent member was the elder Gopāl. Sarat spent the nights there. In the beginning Sarat, Sashī, Bāburām, Niranjan and Kālī used to visit the monastery every now and then, according to their convenience. Tārak, who had gone to Vrindāvan following the Master's death, returned to Calcutta after a few months and soon became a permanent member of the monastery. Rākhāl, Jogin, Lātu, and Kālī were living at Vrindāvan with the Holy Mother when the monastery was started. Kālī returned to Calcutta within a month. Rākhāl after a few months, and Jogin and Lātu after a year. The householder devotees frequently visited the monastic brothers and spent hours with them in meditation and study.

After a short time Narendra, Rākhāl, Niranjan, S'arat, S'ashi, Bāburām, Jogin, Tārak, Kāli, and Lātu renounced the world for good. Sāradāprasanna and Subodh joined them some time later. Gangādhar, who was very much attached to Narendra, visited the math regularly. It was he who taught the brothers the hymn sung at the evening service in the S'iva temple at Benares. He had gone to Tibet to practise austerity; now, having returned he lived at the monastery. Hari at first only visitor at the monastery, soon embraced the monastic life and thus completed the list of the Master's sannyāsi disciples[1].

Surendra was indeed a blessed soul. It was he who laid the foundation of the great order later associated with Sri Rama-krishna's name. His devotion and sacrifice made it possible for those earnest souls to renounce the world for the realization of

[1] The monastic names of the Master's intimate disciples who renounced the world soon after his death were as follows:

Narendra	....	....	Swami Vivekananda
Rakhal	....	....	Swami Brahmananda
Jogin	....	....	Swami Jogananda
Niranjan	....	....	Swami Niranjanananda
Latu	....	....	Swami Adbhutananda
Baburam	....	....	Swami Premananda
Tarak	....	....	Swami Shivananda
Hari	....	....	Swami Turiyananda
S'arat	....	....	Swami Saradananda
S'ashi	....	....	Swami Ramakrishnananda
Kali	....	....	Swami Abhedananda
Gangadhar	....	....	Swami Akhandananda
Gopal (elder)	....	....	Swami Advaitananda
Saradaprasanna	....	....	Swami Trigunātītananda
Subodh	....	....	Swami Subodhananda

God. Through him Sri Ramakrishna made it possible for them to live in the world as embodiments of his teaching, the renunciation of " woman and gold " and the realization of God.

The brothers lived at the math like orphan boys. Sometimes they would not have the money to pay their house-rent ; sometimes they would have no food in the monastery. Surendra would come and settle all these things. He was the big brother of the monks. Later on, when they thought of his genuine love, the members of this first math shed tears of gratitude.

The new monastery became known among the Master's devotees as the Barānagore Math. Narendra, Rākhāl and the other young disciples were filled with intense renunciation. One day Rākhāl's father came to the math and asked Rākhāl to return home. " Why do you take the trouble to come here ? " Rākhāl said to him. " I am very happy here. Please pray to God that you may forget me and that I may forget you too." The young disciples said to each other: " We shall never return to the worldly life. The Master enjoined upon us the renunciation of ' woman and gold ' How can we go back to our families ? "

Sashī had taken charge of the daily worship in the math. The Master's relics had been brought from Balarām's house and Sri Ramakrishna was worshipped daily in the worship hall. Narendra supervised the household. He was the leader of the monastery. He would often tell his brother disciples, " The selfless actions enjoined in the *Gita* are worship, japa, meditation and so on and not worldly duties." The brothers at the math depended on him for their spiritual inspiration. He said to them, " We must practise sādhanā ; otherwise we shall not be able to realize God."

He and his brother disciples, filled with an ascetic spirit, devoted themselves day and night to the practice of spiritual discipline. Their one goal in life was the realization of God. They followed to their hearts' content the injunctions prescribed in the Vedas, Purānas and Tantras for an ascetic life. They spent their time in japa and meditation and study of the scriptures. Whenever they would fail to experience the divine-presence, they would feel as if they were on the rack. They would practise austerity, sometimes alone under trees, sometimes in a cremation ground, sometimes on the bank of the Ganges. Again, sometimes they would spend the entire day in the meditation room of the monastery in japa and contemplation ; sometimes they would gather to sing and dance in a rapture of delight. All of them and Narendra particularly, were consumed with the desire to see God. Now and then they would say to each other, " Shall we not starve ourselves to death to see God ? "

Monday, February 21, 1887

Narendra, Rākhāl, Niranjan, Sarat, Sashī, Kālī, Bāburām, Tārak and Sāradāprasanna were living in the monastery. All day the members had been fasting in observance of the S'ivarātri.[2] Sarat, Kālī, Niranjan, and Sāradā were planning to go to Purī, the following Saturday, on a pilgrimage to the sacred Jagannāth. Jogin and Lātu were at Vrindāvan and had not yet seen the new place.

Narendra had gone to Calcutta that morning to look after a law-suit in which his family had been involved since the death of his father. At nine o'clock in the morning M. arrived at the math. Tārak saw him and began to sing in praise of S'iva, Rākhāl joining him :

---

[2] The night of S'iva. On this day the devotees observe fast and spend the whole night in meditation, prayer, and other spiritual exercises.

There S'iva dances, striking both His cheeks; and they resound, *Ba-ba-bom !*

> *Dimi-dimi-dimi !* sounds His drum; a garland of skulls from His neck is hanging !

> In His matted locks the Ganges hisses; fire shoots from His mighty trident !

> Round His waist a serpent glitters and on His brow the moon is shining!

Rākhāl and Tārak danced as they sang. Narendra had recently composed the song.

S'ashī finished the morning worship in the shrine. S'arat then sang about S'iva to the accompaniment of the tānpurā.

Narendra had just arrived from Calcutta. He had not yet taken his bath. Kālī asked him, "What about the law suit?" "Why should you bother about it?" Narendra replied sharply.

Narendra was smoking and talking to M. and the others. He said: "Nothing can be achieved in spiritual life without the renunciation of 'woman and gold'. 'Woman' is the doorway to hell. All people are under the control of women. The cases of S'iva and Krishna are quite different. S'iva turned His consort into His servant. Sri Krishna, no doubt, led a householder's life. But how unattached He was! How quickly He renounced Vrindāvan and the gopis!"

RĀKHĀL: "And how He renounced Dwārakā, too, where He was king!"

Narendra took his bath in the Ganges and returned to the monastery. He carried his wet cloth and towel in his hand. Sāradā prostrated himself before Narendra. He too had been fasting on account of the S'ivaratri. He was going to the Ganges for his bath. Narendra entered the worship room and prostrated himself before the picture of Sri Ramakrishna, who was daily worshipped there as the Deity. For a few minutes he was absorbed in meditation.

The devotees assembled in a room and began to converse. The talk turned to Bhavanāth. Narendra said, " People like him live like worms in the world."

It was afternoon. Arrangements were being made to worship S'iva in the evening. Leaves of the bel-tree were gathered for the worship. Bel-wood was chopped for the homa.

In the evening S'ashī, who was in charge of the worship at the monastery, burnt incense before the pictures of the various gods and goddesses.

The worship of S'iva was to take place under the bel-tree in the monastery compound. The Deity was to be worshipped four times, during the four watches of the night. The brothers assembled under the bel-tree. Bhūpati and M. were present also. One of the young members of the math was in charge of the worship. Kālī was reading from the *Gita*. Now and then he argued with Narendra.

KĀLĪ: "I alone am everything. I create, preserve and destroy."

NARENDRA: " How is it possible for me to create? Another power creates through me. Our various actions—even our thoughts—are caused by that power.

M : (*to himself*): " The Master used to say : ' As long as a man feels that it is he who meditates, he is under the jurisdiction of the Ādyās'akti. S'akti must be acknowledged.' "

Kālī reflected in silence a few moments and then said: " The actions you are talking about are illusory. There is not even any such thing as thought. The very idea of these things makes me laugh."

NARENDRA : " The 'I' that is implied in ' I am He' is not this ego. It is that which remains after one eliminates mind, body and so on."

After completing the recital of the *Gita*, Kālī chanted: " Sāntih ! Sāntih ! Sāntih ! "

Narendra and the other devotees stood up and circled round and round the tree, singing and dancing. Now and then they chanted in chorus : " Siva Guru ! Siva Guru ! "

It was midnight, the fourteenth day of the dark fortnight of the moon. Pitch darkness filled all the quarters. Men, birds and animals were all hushed into silence. The young sannyāsīs were clad in gerruā robes. The words " Siva Guru ", chanted in their full-throated voices, rose into the infinite sky like the rumblings of rain-clouds and disappeared in the indivisible Satchidānanda.

The worship was over. The sun, about to rise, was painting the eastern horizon crimson. In this sacred twilight, the conjunction of night and day, the holy Brāhmamuhurta, the young worshippers finished their baths in the Ganges.

It was morning. The devotees went to the shrine room, prostrated themselves before the Deity and gradually assembled in the big hall. Narendra was clad in a new ochre cloth. The bright orange colour of his apparel blended with the celestial lustre of his face and body, every pore of which radiated a divine light. His countenance was filled with fiery brilliance and yet touched with the tenderness of love. He appeared to all as a bubble that had risen up in the ocean of absolute Existence and Bliss and assumed a human body to help in the propagation of his Master's message. All eyes were fixed on him. Narendra was then just twenty-four years old, the very age at which the great Chaitanya had renounced the world.

Balarām had sent fruit and sweets to the monastery for the devotees' breakfast. Rākhāl, Narendra and a few others partook of the refreshments. After eating one or two morsels some of them cried out, "Blessed indeed is Balarām!" All laughed.

Narendra now began to joke like a child. He was imitating Sri Ramakrishna. He put a sweet into his mouth and stood still, as if in samādhi. His eyes remained unwinking. A devotee stepped forward and pretended to hold him up by the hand lest he should drop to the ground. Narendra closed his eyes. A few minutes later, with the sweetmeat still in his mouth, he opened his eyes and drawled out, "I—am—all—right." All laughed loudly.

Refreshments were now given to everyone. M. looked on at this wonderful mart of happiness. The devotees shouted joyfully, "Jai Gurumahārāj!"[3]

Monday, March 25, 1887

M. arrived at the Barānagore Math to visit his brother disciples. Devendra accompanied him. M. had been coming to the monastery very frequently and now and then had spent a day or two. The previous week he had spent three days at the math. He was very eager to observe the spirit of intense renunciation of these young men.

It was evening. M. intended to spend the night in the monastery. S'ashī lighted the lamp in the worship room and chanted the name of God. Next he burnt incense before all the

[3] Victory to the Guru.

pictures of gods and goddesses in the various rooms. The evening service began. S'ashī conducted the worship. The members of the math, with M. and Devendra, stood with folded hands and sang the hymn of the ārati.

When the worship was over, Narendra and M. became engaged in conversation. Narendra was recalling his various meetings with Sri Ramakrishna.

NARENDRA: "One day, during one of my early visits, the Master in an ecstatic mood said to me, 'You have come!' 'How amazing!' I said to myself. 'It is as if he had known me a long time.' Then he said to me, 'Do you ever see light?' I replied: 'Yes, sir. Before I fall asleep I feel something like a light revolving near my forehead.'"

M: "Do you see it even now?"

NARENDRA: "I used to see it frequently. In Jadu Mallicks's garden-house the Master one day touched me and muttered something to himself. I became unconscious. The effect of the touch lingered with me a month, like an intoxication.

"When he heard that a proposal had been made about my marriage, he wept, holding the feet of the image of Kāli. With tears in his eyes he prayed to the divine Mother: 'O Mother, please upset the whole thing! Don't let Narendra be drowned.'

"After my father's death my mother and my brothers were starving. When the Master met Annadā Guha one day, he said to him: 'Narendra's father has died. His family is in a state of great privation. It would be good if his friends helped him now with money.'

"After Annadā had left I scolded him. I said, 'Why did you say all those things to him?' Thus rebuked, he wept and said, 'Alas! for your sake I could beg from door to door.'

" He tamed us by his love.   Don't you think so ? "

M :   "There is not the slightest doubt about it. His love was utterly unselfish."

NARENDRA : " One day when I was alone with him he said something to me. Nobody else was present. Please don't repeat it to anyone here."

M :   " No, I shall not.   What did he say ? "

NARENDRA : "He said: 'It is not possible for me to exercise occult powers; but I shall do so through you. What do you say? ' ' No ' I replied, ' you can't do that.'

" I used to laugh at his words. You must have heard all these things from him. I told him that his visions of God were·all hallucinations of his mind.

" He said to me :   ' I used to climb to the roof of the kuthī and cry : " O devotees, where are you all ? Come to me, O devotees ! I am about to die. I shall certainly die if I do not see you." And the divine Mother told me, " The devotees will come." You see, everything is turning out to be true.'

" What else could I say ?   I kept quiet.

" One day he closed the door of his room and said to Devendra Bābu and Girish Bābu, referring to me, ' He will not keep his body if he is told who he is.' "

M :   " Yes, we have heard that. Many a time he repeated the same thing to us, too. Once you came to know about your true Self in nirvikalpa samādhi at the Cossipore garden house. Isn't that true ?"

NARENDRA : " Yes. In that experience I felt that I had no body. I could see only my face. The Master was in the upstairs room. I had that experience downstairs. I was weeping. I said, ' What has happened to me ? ' The elder Gopāl went to the Master's room and said, ' Narendra is crying.'

" When I saw the Master he said to me : ' Now you have known. But I am going to keep the key with me.'

" I said to him, ' What is it that happened to me ? '

" Turning to the devotees, he said : ' He will not keep his body if he knows who he is. But I have put a veil over his eyes.'

" One day he said to me, ' You can see Krishna in your heart if you want.' I replied, ' I don't believe in Krishna or any such nonsense ! ' (*Both M. and Narendra laugh.*)

" I have noticed a peculiar thing. Some men, objects or places make me feel as if I had seen them before, in a previous birth. They appear familiar to me. One day I went to S'arat's house in Calcutta, on Amherst Street. Immediately I said to S'arat : ' This house seems familiar to me. It seems to me that I have known the rooms, the passages and the rest of the house for many, many days.

" I used to follow my own whims in everything I did. The Master never interfered. You know that I became a member of the Sādhāran Brāhmo Samāj."

M : " Yes, I know that."

NARENDRA : " The Master knew that women attended the meetings of the Brahmo Samāj. A man cannot meditate with women sitting in front of him ; therefore he criticized the meditation of the Brāhmo Samāj. But he didn't object to my going there. But one day he said to me, ' Don't tell Rākhāl about your being a member of the Brāhmo Samāj, or he too will feel like becoming one.' "

M : " You have greater strength of mind. That is why the Master didn't prevent your going to the Samaj."

NARENDRA : " I have attained my present state of mind as a result of much suffering and pain. You have not passed through any such suffering. I now realize that without trials and tribulations one cannot resign oneself to God and depend on Him absolutely.

" Well, X—is so modest and humble! He is totally self-effacing. Can you tell me how I can develop humility ? "

M : " Speaking about your ego, the Master said, ' Whose ego is it ? "

NARENDRA : " What did he mean ? "

M : " A friend one day said to Rādhikā : ' You are egotistic. That is why you insulted Krishna. Whereupon another friend said to the first : ' Yes, Radhikā is egotistic, no doubt. But whose ego is it ? ' What she meant was that Rādhā was egotistic because she regarded Krishna as her Lord. It was Krishna Himself who kept that ego in Rādhā.

" What the Master meant was that it is God alone who has kept this ego in you, so that He may accomplish many things through you."

NARENDRA : " But my ego loudly proclaims to all that I have no suffering."

M : (smiling) : " You may loudly proclaim it, if that be your sweet will."

The conversation turned to other devotees.

NARENDRA : " The Master said about Vijay Goswāmī, ' He is knocking at the door.' "

M : " That is to say, he has not yet entered the room. At S'yāmpukur Vijay said to the Master, 'I saw you at Dāccā in this tangible form, in this very body.' You were there too."

NARENDRA : " Devendra Bābu and Ram Bābu want to renounce the world. They are trying hard. Ram Bābu told me privately that he would give up the world after two years."

M : " After two years ? After making provision for his children ? "

NARENDRA : " Besides, he will rent his present house and buy a small house. Other relatives will arrange his daughter's marriage."

M : " Gopāl[4] is in an exalted state of mind, isn't he ? "

NARENDRA : " What do you mean ? "

M : " So much emotion, so much weeping and such exaltation in the name of God ! "

NARENDRA : " Does mere emotion make a man spiritually great ? Youngsters like Kālī, S'arat, S'ashī, and Sāradā are more spiritual than Gopāl. How great their renunciation is ! Gopāl does not accept the Master, does he ? "

M : " That is true. The Master remarked that Gopāl did not belong to the circle of his devotees. But I saw him show great reverence for Sri Ramakrishna."

NARENDRA : " What did you see ? "

M : " At that time I was just becoming acquainted with Sri Ramakrishna. One day, after the meeting of the devotees in his room had broken up, I came out and saw Gopāl on the foot-

---

4 Referring to Nityagopāl.

R—10

path, kneeling with folded hands before the Master. The moon was shining brightly overhead. It was the red path sprinkled with brick-dust, just outside the long verandah north of the Master's room. Nobody else was there. It appeared to me that Gopāl had taken shelter at Sri Ramakrishna's feet and the Master was encouraging him."

NARENDRA: "I didn't see it."

M: "Further, the Master used to say, 'Gopāl is in the state of a paramahamsa.' But I also distinctly remember his forbidding Gopāl to be intimate with woman devotees. Many a time he warned him about it."

NARENDRA: "Speaking to me about Gopāl, the Master asked why, if Gopāl was a real paramahamsa, he should hanker after money. 'He doesn't belong to this place', the Master said. 'Those who are my own will always come here.' He used to be angry with T—because he was Gopāl's constant companion and didn't come to the Master more often. 'Gopāl has spiritual realizations, no doubt,' the Master said to me, 'but he has attained them all of a sudden, without the necessary preparations. He is not one of my own. If he is, why haven't I wept for him?'

"Some are proclaiming Gopāl as the reincarnation of Nityānanda. But times without number the Master said to me: 'In me alone are embodied Advaita, Chaitanya, and Nityānanda.[5] I am all these three.'"

Friday, April 8, 1887

About eight o'clock in the morning two devotees, one a householder and the other a monk, were conversing in a room in the Baranagore monastery, when M. came in. The devotees were

---

[5] Advaita and Nityānanda were intimate companions of Chaitanya.

of the same age—twenty-four or twenty-five years old. M. intended to spend three days at the monastery. He went to the shrine and saluted the Deity. After visiting Narendra, Rākhāl, and the other brothers, he at last came into the room where the two devotees were engaged in conversation. The householder devotee wanted to renounce the world. The monk was trying to persuade him not to do so.

M : " Why don't you finish the few duties you have in the world ? Very soon they will be left behind.

" A man was told that he would go to hell. He asked a friend, ' What is hell like ? ' Thereupon the friend began to draw a picture of hell on the ground with a piece of chalk. No sooner was the picture drawn than the man rolled over it and said, ' Now I have gone through hell ! ' "

HOUSEHOLDER : " I don't relish worldly life. Ah, how happy you are here ! "

M : " Why don't you renounce the world, if you want to ? Why do you talk about it so much ? But I repeat, why don't you enjoy the fun once for all ? "

S'ashī finished the regular worship in the worship-hall. About eleven the brothers of the math returned from the Ganges after taking their baths. They put on clean cloths, went to the shrine, prostrated themselves before the Deity, and meditated there a little while.

After the food was offered to the Deity they had their meal. M. ate with them.

It was evening. Incense was burnt before the pictures of gods and goddesses and the evening service was performed. Rākhāl, S'ashī, the elder Gopāl, and Harish were seated in the big hall. M. also was there. Rākhāl warned one of the brothers to be careful about the food to be offered to the Master in the shrine.

RĀKHĀL (to S'ashi and the others): "One day I ate part of his [meaning the Master's] refreshments before he took them. At this he said: 'I cannot look at you. How could you do such a thing?' I burst into tears."

THE ELDER GOPĀL: "One day at Cossipore I breathed hard on his food. At this he said, 'Take that food away.'"

M. and Narendra were pacing the verandah and recalling old times.

NARENDRA: "I did not believe in anything."

M: "You mean the forms of God?"

NARENDRA: "At first I did not accept most of what the Master said. One day he asked me, 'Then why do you come here?' I replied, 'I come here to see you, not to listen to you.'"

M: "What did he say to that?"

NARENDRA: "He was very much pleased."

Saturday, April 9, 1887

The members of the math were resting a little after their meal. Narendra and M. sat under a tree in the garden to the west of the monastery. It was a solitary place and no one else was present. Narendra was recounting to M. his various experiences with Sri Ramakrishna. Narendra was about twenty-four years old and M. thirty-two.

M: "You must remember vividly your first visit to him."

NARENDRA: "Yes. It was at the temple garden at Dakshineswar, in his own room. That day I sang two songs."

NARENDRA sang them for M.

> Let us go back once more, O mind, to our own abode!
> Here in this foreign land of earth
> Why should we wander aimlessly in stranger's guise?
> These living beings round about and the five elements,
> Are strangers to you, all of them; none is your own.
> Why do you thus forget yourself,
> In love with strangers, O my mind?
> Why do you thus forget your own?
> Ascend the path of truth, O mind! Unflaggingly climb,
> With love as the lamp to light your way.
> As your provision for the journey, bring with you
> The virtues, carefully concealed; for, like two highwaymen
> Greed and delusion wait to rob you of your wealth.
> And keep beside you constantly,
> As guards to shelter you from harm,
> Calmness of mind and self-control.
> Companionship with holy men will be for you
> A welcome rest-house by the road;
> There rest your weary limbs awhile, asking your way,
> If ever you should be in doubt, of him who watches there.
> If anything along the path should frighten you,
> Then loudly shout the name of the Lord
> For He is ruler of that road,
> And even Death must bow to Him.

*   *   *

> O Lord, must all my days pass by so utterly in vain?
> Down the path of hope I gaze with longing, day and night.
> Thou art the Lord of all the worlds, and I but a beggar here;
> How can I ask of Thee to come and dwell within my heart

My poor heart's humble cottage door is standing open wide ;
Be gracious, Lord, and enter there but once, and quench its
thirst !

M : " What did he say after listening to your songs ?"

NARENDRA : " He went into samādhi. He said to Ram
Bābu : 'Who is this boy ? How well he sings !' He asked me
to come again."

M : " Where did you see him next ?"

NARENDRA : " At Rājmohan's house. The third visit
was at Dakshineswar again. During that visit he went into
samādhi and began to praise me as if I were God. He said
to me, 'O Nārāyana, you have assumed this body for my sake.'
But please don't tell this to anybody else."

M : " What else did he say ?"

NARENDRA : " He said : 'You have assumed this body
for my sake. I asked the divine Mother, " Mother, unless I enjoy
the company of some genuine devotees completely free from
' woman and gold', how shall I live on earth ?"' Then he said
to me, 'You came to me at night, woke me up, and said, " Here
I am !" ' But I did not know anything of this. I was sound
asleep in our Calcutta house."

M : " In other words, you may be both present and absent
at the same time. It is like God, who is both formless and
endowed with form."

NARENDRA : " But you must not tell this to anyone
else. At Cossipore he transmitted his power to me."

M : " Didn't it happen when you used to meditate before
a lighted fire under a tree at the Cossipore garden house ?"

NARENDRA: "Yes. One day, while meditating, I asked Kālī to hold my hand. Kālī said to me 'When I touched your body I felt something like an electric shock coming to my body.'

"But you must not tell this to anybody here. Give me your promise."

M: "There is a special purpose in his transmission of power to you. He will accomplish much work through you. One day the Master wrote on a piece of paper, 'Naren will teach people.'"

NARENDRA: "But I said to him, 'I won't do any such thing.' Thereupon he said, 'Your very bones will do it.' He has given me charge of S'arat. S'arat is now yearning for God; the Kundalini is awakened in him."

M: "He must be careful that dead leaves do not accumulate there. Perhaps you remember what the Master used to say: 'In a lake the fish make holes so that they may rest there. But if dead leaves accumulate in the holes the fish do not go there.'"

NARENDRA: "The Master used to call me Nārāyana."

M: "Yes, I know he did."

NARENDRA: "When he was ill he would not allow me to pour water to wash his hands. At Cossipore he said: 'Now the key is in my hands. He will give up his body when he knows who he is.'"

M: "Didn't he say it when you were in nirvikalpa samādhi?"

NARENDRA: "Yes. At the time it seemed to me I had no body. I felt only my face.

"I was studying law at home to prepare for the examinations. Suddenly I said to myself, 'What am I doing?'"

M : " Didn't it happen when the Master was at Cossipore ?"

NARENDRA : " Yes. Like an insane person I ran out of our house. He asked me, ' What do you want ?' I replied, ' I want to remain immersed in samādhi.' He said : 'What a small mind you have! Go beyond samādhi! Samādhi is a very trifling thing "

M : " Yes, he used to say that vijnāna is the stage after jnāna. It is like going up and down the stairs after reaching the roof."

NARENDRA : " Kālī has a craving for knowledge. I scold him for that. Is knowledge so easy to get ? Let his bhakti first mature. The Master told Tārak at Dakshineswar that emotion and bhakti are by no means the last word."

M : " What other things did he say about you ?"

NARENDRA : " Once I said to him, ' The forms of God and things like that, which you see in your visions, are all figments of your imagination.' He had so much faith in my words that he went to the divine Mother in the temple and told Her what I had said to him. He asked Her, ' Are these hallucinations, then ?' Afterwards he said to me, 'Mother told me that all these are real.'

" Perhaps you remember that he said to me, ' When you sing, He who dwells here (*touching his heart*), like a snake, hisses as it were, and then, spreading His hood, quietly holds Himself steady and listens to your music.'

" He has no doubt said many things about me ; but what have I realized ?"

M : " Now you have put on the garb of S'iva; you cannot touch money. Do you remember the Master's story ?"

NARENDRA : " Please tell it to me."

M: "A vahurupī[6] disguised himself as S'iva and visited a house. The master of the house wanted to give him a rupee, but he did not accept it. Then the mendicant went home, removed his disguise, came back to the gentleman and asked for the rupee. 'Why didn't you accept it before?' he was asked. He said: 'I was impersonating S'iva, a sannyāsī. I couldn't touch money at that time.'"

When Narendra heard the story he laughed a long while.

M: "You have now put on the garb of a physician, as it were. You have become the guardian of these young men. Yours is the entire responsibility. You have to bring up the brothers of the monastery."

NARENDRA: "Whatever spiritual disciplines we are practising here are in obedience to the Master's command. But it is strange that Ram Bābu criticizes us, for our spiritual practices. He says: 'We have seen him.[7] What need have we of any such practice?'"

M: "Let people act according to their faith."

NARENDRA: "But the Master asked us to practise sādhanā."

Narendra was again telling M. about the Master's love for him.

NARENDRA: "How many times he prayed to the divine Mother for my sake! After my father's death, when I had no food at home and my mother and sisters and brothers were starving too, the Master prayed to the divine Mother to give me money."

M: "Yes, I know that. You once told me."

---

6 A professional impersonator.
7 Sri Ramakrishna.

NARENDRA: "But I didn't get any money. The Master told me what the divine Mother had said to him: 'He will get simple food and clothing. He will eat rice and dāl.'

"He loved me so much! But whenever an impure idea crept into my mind he at once knew about it. While going around with Annadā, sometimes I found myself in the company of evil people. On those occasions the Master could not eat any food from my hands. He could raise his hand only a little, and could not bring it to his mouth. On one such occasion, while he was ill, he brought his hand very close to his mouth, but it did not go in. He said to me, 'You are not yet ready.'

"Now and then I feel great scepticism. At Bāburām's house it seemed to me that nothing existed—as if there were no such thing as God."

M: "The Master used to say that he too had passed through that mood."

Both M. and Narendra remained silent. Then M. said: "You are all indeed blessed! You think of the Master day and night."

NARENDRA: "But how little it is! We don't yet feel like giving up the body because we haven't realized God."

It was night. Niranjan had just returned from Purī. The members of the math and M., greeted him with great joy. Niranjan was telling them his experiences. He was then about twenty-five years old.

The evening worship was over. Some of the brothers were meditating. But many of them assembled in the big hall around Niranjan. They were talking. After nine o'clock S'ashī offered food to the Deity.

The members of the math finished their supper, which consisted of home-made bread, a little vegetable and a little hard molasses.

Saturday, May 7, 1887

It was the full-moon day of the month of Vais'ākh. Narendra and M. were seated on a couch in M.'s study in Calcutta. They were talking. Just before Narendra's arrival M. had been studying *The Merchant of Venice*, *Comus* and Blackie's *Self-culture*, which he taught at school.

Narendra and the other brothers of the monastery were full of yearning for God-realization. A fire of intense renunciation raged in their hearts.

NARENDRA: "I don't care for anything. You see, I am now talking with you, but I feel like getting up this minute and running away."

Narendra sat in silence a few minutes. Then he said, "I shall fast to death for the realization of God."

M: "That is good. One can do anything for God."

NARENDRA: "But suppose I cannot control my hunger."

M: "Then eat something and begin over again."

Narendra remained silent a few minutes.

NARENDRA: "It seems there is no God. I pray so much, but there is no reply—none whatsoever.

"How many visions I have seen! How many mantras shining in letters of gold! How many visions of the Goddess Kāli! How many other divine forms! But still I have no peace.

"Will you kindly give me six pice?"

Narendra asked for the money to pay his carriage hire to the Barānagore Math. Just then Śātkari arrived in a carriage. Of the same age as Narendra, he dearly loved the members of the monastery. He lived near the math and worked in Calcutta. The carriage was his own. Narendra returned the money to M. and said that he would go with Sātkari in his carriage. He asked M. to give them some refreshments.

M. accompanied the two friends to the Barānagore Math. He wanted to see how the brothers spent their time and practised sādhanā. He wanted to see how Sri Ramakrishna, the Master, was reflected in the hearts of the disciples. Niranjan was not at the math. He had gone home to visit his mother, the only relative he had in the world. Bāburām, S'arat and Kāli had gone to Puri. They intended to spend a few days there.

Narendra was in charge of the members of the monastery. Prasanna[8] had been practising austere sādhanā for the past few days. Once Narendra had told him of his desire to fast to death for the realization of God. During Narendra's absence in Calcutta, Prasanna had left the monastery for an unknown destination. When Narendra heard about it, he said to the brothers, "Why did Raja[9] allow him to go?" But Rākhāl had not been in the monastery at the time, having gone to the Dakshineswar temple for a stroll.

NARENDRA: "Just let Raja come back to the monastery! I shall scold him. Why did he allow Prasanna to go away?

---

8 Saradāprasanna, one of the Master's young disciples, was addressed as Prasanna by Sri Ramakrishna and his disciples.

9 Rākhāl was addressed as "Raja" by all the brothers. "Rakhal-Raj", the "King of the cowherd boys", is one of the names of Sri Krishna, and Sri Ramakrishna often spoke of Rakhal as one of the intimate companions of Krishna.

(*To Harish*) I am sure you were lecturing him then, standing with your feet apart. Couldn't you prevent his going away?"

Harish replied in a very low voice, "Brother Tārak asked him not to go, but still he went away."

NARENDRA (*to M.*): "You see what a lot of trouble I am in! Here, too, I am involved in a world of māyā. Who knows where this boy has gone?"

Rākhāl returned from Dakshineswar. Bhavanāth had accompanied him.

Narendra told Rākhāl about Prasanna's going away from the monastery. Prasanna had left a letter for Narendra. This was the substance of the letter: "I am going to Vrindāvan on foot. It is very risky for me to live here. Here my mind is undergoing a change. Formerly I used to dream about my parents and other relatives. Then I dreamt of woman, the embodiment of māyā. I have suffered twice; I had to go back to my relatives at home. Therefore I am going far away from them. The Master once told me, ' Your people at home are apt to do anything; never trust them.' "

Rākhāl said: "These are the reasons for his going away. Once he remarked: ' Narendra often goes home to look after his mother, brothers and sisters. And he supervises the family's lawsuit. I am afraid that I too may feel like going home, following his example.' "

Narendra remained silent.

Rākhāl was talking to them about making pilgrimages. He said: "We have achieved nothing by staying here. The Master always exhorted us to realize God. Have we succeeded?"

Rākhāl lay down. The other devotees were either lying down or sitting.

RĀKHĀL: "Let us go to the Narmadā."

NARENDRA: "What will you achieve by wandering about? Can one ever attain jnāna, that you are talking about it so much?"

A DEVOTEE: "Then why have you renounced the world?"

NARENDRA: "Must we live with Shyām because we have not seen Ram? Must we go on begetting children because we have not realized God? What are you talking about?"

Narendra went out, returning after a few minutes. Rākhāl was still lying down.

A member of the monastery who was also lying down said teasingly, feigning great suffering on account of his separation from God: "Ah! Please get me a knife. I have no more use for this life. I can't stand this pain any more!"

NARENDRA: (*feigning seriousness*): "It is there. Stretch out your hand and take it."

Everybody laughed.

The conversation again turned to Prasanna.

NARENDRA: "Even here we are involved in māyā. Why have we become sannyāsīs, I wonder?"

RĀKHĀL: "I have read in a book that sannyāsīs should not live together. The author has described a city of sannyāsīs."

S'ASHĪ: "I don't care about sannyās or any such thing. There is no place where I cannot live."

They were talking of Bhavanāth, whose wife had been seriously ill. Narendra said to Rākhāl: "I understand that his wife has been snatched from the jaws of death. Is that why he went to Dakshineswar to enjoy the fresh air?"

Ram Bābu intended to build a temple in the garden at Kānkurgāchi, where some of Sri Ramakrishna's ashes were buried.

NARENDRA: (to Rākhāl): "Ram Bābu has made M. one of the trustees of the garden."

M: (to Rākhāl): "But I don't know anything about it."

It was dusk. S'ashī burnt incense before the picture of Sri Ramakrishna in the worship room and then before the pictures of gods and goddesses in the other rooms.

The evening worship began. The members of the math and the other devotees stood with folded hands near the door of the shrine and witnessed the ārati. Then they all sang in chorus the following hymn to S'iva, to the accompaniment of bell and gong.

> Jaya S'iva Omkāra, Bhaja S'iva Omkāra,
> Brahmā Vishnu Sadāśiva,
> Hara Hara Hara Mahādeva!

Narendra had introduced this song for the evening worship. It is sung in the temple of S'iva in Bānārās.

It was eleven o'clock at night when their supper was over. The brothers prepared a bed for M. and all went to sleep.

It was midnight. M. was wide awake. He said to himself: "Everything is as it was before. The same Ayodhyā—only Rāma is not there." M. silently left his bed. It was the full-moon night of Vaisākh, the thrice-blessed day of the Buddhists, associated with Buddha's birth, realization and passing away. M. was walking alone on the bank of the Ganges, contemplating the Master.

It was Sunday. M. had arrived the day before and was planning to stay till Wednesday. The householder devotees generally visited the monastery on Sundays.

The *Yogavās'ishtha* was being studied and explained. M. had heard a little about the teachings of this book from Sri Ramakrishna. It taught the absolute identity of Brahman and the soul and the unreality of the world. The Master had forbidden him and the other householder devotees to practise spiritual discipline following the method of the Advaita Vedanta, since the attiude of the oneness of the soul and God is harmful for one still identified with the body. For such a devotee, the Master used to say, it was better to look on God as the Lord and oneself as His servant.

The conversation turned to the *Yogavās'ishtha*.

M: "Well, how is Brahmajnāna described in the *Yogavās'ishtka?*"

RĀKHĀL: "Hunger, thirst, pain, pleasure and so on, are all māyā. The annihilation of the mind is the only means to the realization of Brahman."

M: "What remains after the annihilation of the mind is Brahman. Is that not true?"

RĀKHĀL: "Yes."

M: "Sri Ramakrishna used to say that. Nāngtā taught him that way. Have you found in the book that Vas'ishtha asked Rama to lead a householder's life?"

RĀKHĀL: "I haven't yet found anything like that in the book. Rama is not even admitted by the author ·to be an Incarnation·of God."

Presently Narendra, Tārak and another devotee returned from the bank of the Ganges. They had intended to go to Konnagar, on the other side of the river, but had been unable to find a ferry-boat. They sat down. The conversation about the *Yogavās'ishtha* went on.

NARENDRA: (*to M.*): "There are many nice stories in the book. Do you know the incident of Līlā ?"

M: "Yes, I have read the book here and there. Līlā had attained Brahmajnāna."

NARENDRA: "Yes, Do you remember the story of Indra and Ahalyā, and the story of how king Viduratha became a chandāla?"

M: "Yes, I remember."

NARENDRA: "What a wonderful description of the forest?"

Narendra and the other devotees were going to the Ganges to bathe. M. accompanied them. The sun was very hot; so M. took his umbrella. S'arat, a devotee from Barānagore, was going with them to take his bath. He often visited the monastery.

M. (*to S'arat*): "It is very hot."

NARENDRA: "Is that your excuse for taking the umbrella?"

M: laughed.

The members of the monastery were clad in gerruā.

M. (*to Narendra*): "It is really very hot. One is liable to get a sunstroke."

NARENDRA: "I see that your body is the obstacle in your path of renunciation. Isn't that so? I mean you, Devendra Bābu—"

M: laughed and said to himself, "Is it merely the body?"

R—11

After bathing, the devotees returned to the monastery. They washed their feet and entered the worship room. Saluting the Deity, they offered flowers.

Narendra was a little late in coming to the worship room. He found that there was no flower on the tray. There were only a few bel-leaves. He sprinkled the leaves with sandal-paste and offered them to Sri Ramakrishna. He rang the bell, saluted the Deity again and joined the other brothers in the big hall, which was known as the room of the "dānās."

The members of the math called themselves the "dānās" and the "daityas", which mean the "ghosts" and the "demons", the companions of S'iva. They took these names because of their utter indifference to worldly pleasures and relationships.

The southernmost room of the second floor was used for meditation, contemplation and study and was known as Kālī Tapasvī's room, since Kālī used to shut himself in there most of the day. North of this room was the worship room and north of that, again, was the room where the offerings for the worship were prepared. From this room the devotees used to watch the evening worship. North of the "offering room" was the room of the "dānās", a very long hall where the members of the math used to assemble. Here the householder devotees and visitors were received. North of this hall was a small room where the devotees took their meals. East of the worship room and of Kālī Tapasvī's room ran a long verandah, at the south-west corner of which was the library of a society of Baranāgore. Between Kālī Tapasvī's room and this library was a staircase; and north of the dining-room was another staircase, leading to the roof.

Narendra and the other members of the math often spent their evenings on this roof. There they devoted a great deal of time to discussion of the teachings of Sri Ramakrishna;

S'ankarāchārya, Rāmānuja and Jesus Christ and of Hindu philosophy, European philosophy, the Vedas, the Purānas and the Tantras.

Narendra, who had a beautiful voice, used to sing in the room of the " dānās " and teach music to S'arat and a few others. Kālī used to take lessons on the instruments. Many, many happy hours they spent together in that hall, dancing and singing.

Narendra was sitting with the devotees in the room of the " dānās." The conversation turned to religious preaching.

M. (to Narendra): " Vidyāsāgar says that he does not speak about God to anyone for fear of being caned."

NARENDRA: " For fear of being caned? What does he mean ?"

M: " This is what Vidyāsāgar says: ' Suppose that after death we all go to God. The emissaries of Death will have sent Keshab Sen there too. Keshab Sen, no doubt, committed sins while he lived on earth. When that is proved, perhaps God will say, " Give him twenty-five stripes." Then suppose I am taken to God. I used to go to Keshab Sen's Brāhmo Samāj in my earthly life. I too have committed many sins; so I too am ordered to be caned. Then suppose I say to God that I acted in that sinful way because I listened to Keshab's preaching. Thereupon God will ask His emissaries to bring Keshab back. When he is brought, the Almighty Lord will say to him : " Did you really preach that way ? You yourself knew nothing about spiritual matters and yet you had the hardihood to teach others about God! Emissaries! Give him twenty-five stripes more."

Everybody laughed.

M: " Therefore Vidyāsagār says: ' I cannot take care of my ownself; should I be foolish enough to get an additional caning for misleading others? I myself do not understand God. How shall I lecture to others about Him?'"

NARENDRA: "How has he—who could not understand God—understood other things?"

M: "What other things?"

NARENDRA: "He says that he has not understood God. But how, then, can he understand charity and doing good to others? How can he understand about the school? How can he understand about educating boys by establishing schools? How can he understand that it is right to enter the world, marry and beget children?

"He who rightly understands one thing understands everything else."

M: (*to himself*): "Yes, Sri Ramakrishna, too, said that he who knows God knows everything else. Further, he said to Vidyāsagār that leading a worldly life, establishing schools, and so on are the outcome of rajas. The Master also said that Vidyāsāgar's philanthropy was due to the influence of sattva on rajas. Such rajas is not harmful."

After their meal the brothers of the monastery rested. M. and Chūnilāl were conversing. Chūnilāl told M. of his first visit to Sri Ramakrishna at Dakshineswar. He also told him how at one time he had felt disgusted with the world, had renounced it and had wandered about in holy places. A few minutes later Narendra came and sat by them. He asked the younger Gopāl to prepare a smoke for him. The latter had been meditating. Narendra said to him: "I say! Prepare a smoke. What do you mean by this meditation? First of all prepare yourself for spiritual life by serving God and holy men; then you will be able to meditate. First of all karma, and then meditation." Everybody laughed.

There was a big plot of wooded land to the west of the monastery compound. M. was seated alone under a tree, when suddenly Prasanna appeared. It was about three o'clock in the afternoon.

M: "Where have you been all these days? Everyone has been so worried about you. Have you seen the brothers? When did you arrive?"

PRASANNA: "Just now. Yes, I have seen them."

M: "You left a note saying that you were going to Vrindāvan. We were terribly worried about you. How far did you go?"

PRASANNA: "Only as far as Konnagar."[10]

Both of them laughed.

M. "Sit down. Tell me all about it. Where did you stop first?"

PRASANNA: "At the Dakshineswar temple garden. I spent one night there."

M. (*smiling*): "What is Hāzrā's present mood?"

PRASANNA: "Hāzrā asked me, 'What do you think of me?'"

Both laughed.

M: (*smiling*): "What did you say?"

PRASANNA: "I said nothing."

M: "Then?"

PRASANNA: "Then he asked me whether I had brought tobacco for him."

---

10 A small town only a few miles from Baranagore, on the other side of the Ganges.

Both laughed.

PRASANNA : " He wanted me to wait on him." (*Laughter.*)

M : " Where did you go next ? "

PRASANNA : " By degrees I got to Konnagar. I spent the night in the open. I intended to proceed farther and asked some gentlemen whether I could procure enough money there for a railway ticket to the up-country."

M : " What did they say ? "

PRASANNA : " They said, ' You may get a rupee or so; but who will give you the whole fare ? '"

Both laughed.

M : " What did you take with you ? "

PRASANNA : " Oh, one or two pieces of cloth and a picture of the Master. I didn't show the picture to anybody."

S'ashī's father came to the math. He wanted to take his son home. During Srī Ramakrishna's illness S'ashī had nursed the Master for nine months with unswerving zeal. He had won a scholarship in the Entrance Examination for his academic ability and had studied up to the B.A., but he had not appeared at the examination. His father, a poor Brāhmin, was a devout Hindu and spent much of his time in spiritual practice. S'ashī was his eldest son. His parents had hoped that, after completing his education, he would earn money and remove the family's financial difficulties. But S'ashī had renounced the world for the realization of God. Whenever he thought of his father and mother he felt great anguish of heart. Many a time he said to his friends, with tears in his eyes: " I am at a loss as to my duty. Alas, I could not serve my parents ; I could not be of any use to them. What great hope they placed in me! On account of our poverty my mother did not have any jewelry. I cherished the desire to buy some for her. But now all my hopes are frustrated; it is impossible for me to return home. My Master asked me to renounce ' woman and gold'. I simply cannot return home."

After Sri Ramakrishna's passing away S'ashi's father had hoped that his son would come back to his family. The boy had spent a few days at home, but immediately after the establishment of the new monastery he had begun to frequent it and after a few days, had decided to remain there as one of the members. Every now and then his father came to the monastery to persuade him to come home; but he had not succeeded.

This day, on learning that his father had come, S'ashi fled the monastery by another door. He did not want to meet him.

S'ashi's father knew M. They paced the upper verandah together and talked.

SASHI'S FATHER : " Who is in charge of this place? Narendra alone is the cause of all the mischief. For a while all these young men returned home and devoted themselves to their studies."

M : " There is no master here. They are all equals. What can Narendra do? Can a man renounce home against his own will? Have we householders, for instance, been able to give up our homes altogether?"

S'ASHI'S FATHER : " You are doing the right thing. You are serving both the world and God. Can't one practise religion after your method? That is exactly what we want S'ashi to do. Let him live at home and come here too. You have no idea how much his mother weeps for him."

M : became sad and said nothing.

S'ASHĪ'S FATHER : " And if you speak of searching for holy men, I know where to find a good one. Let S'ashī go to him."

Rākhāl and M. were walking on the verandah to the east of Kālī Tapasvī's room.

RĀKHĀL (*earnestly*): " M., let us practise sadhanā ! We have renounced home for good. When someone says, ' You have not realized God by renouncing home ; then why all this fuss ?" Narendra gives a good retort. He says, ' Because we could not attain Ram, must we live with Shyām and beget children ?' Ah ! Every now and then Narendra says nice things. You had better ask him."

M : " What you say is right. I see that you too have become restless for God "

RĀKHĀL : " M., how can I describe the state of my mind? Today at noontime I felt great yearning for the Narmadā. M., please practise sādhanā ; otherwise you will not succeed. Even S'ukadeva was afraid of this world. That is why immediately after his birth he fled the world. His father asked him to wait, but he ran straight away. "

M : " Yes, the *Yogopanishad* describes how S'ukadeva fled this world of māyā. It also describes Vyāsa's conversation with S'uka. Vyāsa asked his son to practise religion in the world. But S'uka said that the one essential thing is the lotus feet of God. He also expressed his disgust with worldly men for getting married and living with women."

RĀKHĀL : " Many people think that it is enough not to look at the face of a woman. But what will you gain merely by turning your eyes to the ground at the sight of a woman ? Narendra put it very well last night, when he said : ' Woman exists for a man as long as he has lust. Free from lust, one sees no difference between man and woman."

M: "How true it is! Children do not see the difference between man and woman."

RĀKHĀL: "Therefore I say that we must practise spiritual discipline. How can one attain knowledge without going beyond māyā?

"Let's go to the big hall. Some gentlemen have come from Barānagore. Narendra is talking with them. Let's go and listen to him."

M. did not enter the room. As he was pacing outside he overheard some of the conversation.

NARENDRA: "There is no fixed time or place for the sandhya and other devotions."

GENTLEMAN: "Sir, can one realize God through spiritual practice alone?"

NARENDRA: "Realization depends on God's grace. Sri Krishna says in the *Gita*:

The Lord, O Arjuna, dwells in the hearts of all boings, causing them, by his māyā, to revolve as if mounted on a machine. Take refuge in Him with all thy heart, O Bhārata. By His grace wilt thou attain supreme Peace and the eternal Abode.

"Without the grace of God mere worship and prayer do not help at all. Therefore one should take refuge in Him."

GENTLEMAN: "May we come now and then and disturb you?"

NARENDRA: "Please come whenever you like. We take our baths in the Ganges at your ghāt."

GENTLEMAN: "I don't mind that. But please see that others don't use it."

NARENDRA: "We shall not use your ghāt, if that is what you mean."

GENTLEMAN: "No, I don't mean exactly that. But if you see other people using it, then you had better not go."

It was dusk. The evening worship was over. The devotees, as usual, sang in chorus, "Jaya S'iva Omkāra". Afterwards they assembled in the room of the "dānās". M., too, was seated there. Prasanna was reading from the *Guru Gita*.

Narendra sang:

> I salute the eternal Teacher, who is the embodiment of the bliss of Brahman,
>
> The essence of knowledge and liberation, the giver of supreme Joy;
>
> Who is all-pervading, like the ākās'a and is the goal of Vedānta's teachings;
>
> Who is one, eternal, stainless, pure and is the constant witness of all things;
>
> Who dwells beyond all moods, transcending the three gunas.

Narendra sang again:

> There is none higher than the Guru, none better than the Guru;
> This is what S'iva has declared.
> I shall sing of the blessed Guru, the supreme Brahman;
> I shall worship the blessed Guru, the supreme Brahman;
> I shall meditate on the blessed Guru, the supreme Brahman;
> I shall bow down to the blessed Guru, the supreme Brahman;

As Narendrā sang these verses from the *Guru Gīta* in his melodious voice, the minds of the devotees became steady like a candle-flame in a windless place.

Rākhāl was seated in Kālī Tapasvī's room. Prasanna sat near him. M., too, was there.

Rākhāl had renounced the world, leaving behind his wife and child. A fire of intense renunciation burnt day and night in his heart. He was thinking seriously of going away by himself, to the bank of the Narmadā or some other holy place. Still, he was trying to persuade Prasanna not to run away from the monastery.

RĀKHĀL : (*to Prasanna*): " Where do you want to go, running away from here ? Here you are in the company of holy men. Wouldn't it be foolish to run away from this ? Where will you find another like Narendra ? "

PRASANNA : " My parents live in Calcutta. I am afraid of being drawn by their love. That is why I want to flee to a distant place."

RĀKHĀL : " Can our parents love us as intensely as Guru-mahārāj [meaning Sri Ramakrishna] did ? What have we done for him, to deserve all this love ? Why was he so eager for our welfare in body, mind and soul ? What have we done for him, to deserve all this ? "

M. (*to himself*): " Ah! Rākhāl is right. Therefore a person like Sri Ramakrishna is described as the ' Ocean of Mercy without any reason '."

PRASANNA : (*to Rākhāl*): '' Don't you yourself feel like running away from here ? "

RĀKHĀL : " Yes, now and then I have a fancy to spend a few days on the bank of the Narmadā. I say to myself,

'Let me go to a place like that and practise sādhanā in a garden.' Again, I feel a strong desire to practise the panchatapā for three days. But I hesitate to live in a garden that belongs to worldly people."

Tārak and Prasanna were talking in the room of the "dānās". Tārak had lost his mother. His father, like Rākhāl's father, had married a second time. Tārak himself had married but had lost his wife. Now the monastery was his home. He too was trying to persuade Prasanna to live there.

PRASANNA: "I have neither jnāna nor prema. What have I in the world for a support?"

TĀRAK: "It is no doubt difficult to attain jnāna; but how can you say you have no prema?"

PRASANNA: "I have not yet wept for God. How can I say I have prema? What have I realized in all these days?"

TĀRAK: "But you have seen the Master. And why do you say that you have no jnāna?"

PRASANNA: "What sort of jnāna are you talking about? Jnāna means knowledge. Knowledge of what? Certainly of God. But I am not even sure of the existence of God."

TĀRAK: "Yes, that's true. According to the jnānī, there is no God."

M. (to himself): "Ah! The Master used to say that those who seek God pass through the state that Prasanna is now experiencing. In that state sometimes one doubts the very existence of God. I understand that Tārak is now reading Buddhistic philosophy. That is why he says that according to the jnāni God does not exist. But Sri Ramakrishna used to say that the jnāni and the bhakta will ultimately arrive at the same destination."

Narendra and Prasanna were talking in the meditation room. Rākhāl, Harish and the younger Gopāl were seated in another part of the room. After a while the elder Gopāl came in.

Narendra was reading from the Gita and explaining the verses to Prasanna:

> The Lord, O Arjuna, dwells in the hearts of all beings, causing them, by His māyā, to revolve as if mounted on a machine. Take refuge in Him with all thy heart, O Bhārata. By His grace wilt thou attain supreme Peace and the eternal Abode. Relinquishing all dharmas, take refuge in Me alone. I shall liberate thee from all sins. Grieve not.

NARENDRA: "Did you notice what Krishna said? 'Mounted on a machine.' The Lord, by His māyā, causes all beings to revolve as if mounted on a machine. To seek to know God? You are but a worm among worms—and you to know God? Just reflect a moment: what is a man? It is said that each one of the myriads of stars that shine overhead represents a solar system. This earth of ours is a part of only one solar system and even that is too big for us. Like an insect man walks about on this earth, which, compared to the sun, is only a tiny ball."

Narendra sang:

> We are born, O Lord, in the dust of earth,
> And our eyes are blinded by the dust;
> With dust we toy like children at play:
> O give us assurance, Thou help of the weak!
> Wilt Thou cast us out of Thy lap, O Lord,
> For a single mistake? Wilt Thou turn away
> And abandon us to our helplessness?
> Oh, then we shall never be able to rise,
> But shall lie for ever dazed and undone.

Mere babes are we, Father, with baby minds;
At every step we stumble and fall.
Why, then, must Thou show us Thy terrible face?
Why, Lord, must we ever behold Thy frown?
Small are we—oh, do not be angry with us,
But tenderly speak to us when we do wrong;
For though Thou dost raise us a hundred times,
A hundred times we shall fall again!
What else can one do with a helpless mind?

Then he said to Prasanna: "Surrender yourself at His feet. Resign yourself completely to His will."

Narendra sang again in an ecstatic mood:

O Lord, I am Thy servant, I am Thy servant! Thy servant am I!

O Lord, Thou art my Master, Thou art my Master! My Master art Thou!

From Thee I have received two pieces of bread and a kaupin; [11]

When I sing Thy name, devotion wells up in my heart and shields me from harm.

Thou art the Master, the All-compassionate; this I repeat, O Lord!

Thy servant Kabîr has taken refuge at Thy feet.

Narendra said to Prasanna: "Don't you remember Sri Ramakrishna's words? God is the hill of sugar and you are but an ant. One grain is enough to fill your stomach, and you think of bringing home the entire hill! Don't you remember what the Master said about S'ukadeva? Even S'ukadeva was a big ant at

---

[11] Loin-cloth of a monk.

the most. That is why I scolded Kālī, saying: ' You fool! Do you want to measure God with your tape and foot-rule?'

" God is the ocean of mercy. Be His slave and take refuge in Him. He will show compassion. Pray to Him: ' Protect me always with Thy compassionate face. Lead me from the unreal to the real, from darkness to light, from death to immortality. Reveal Thyself to me and protect me always with Thy compassionate face.' "

PRASANNA : " What kind of spiritual discipline should one practise?"

NARENDRA : " Repeat His name. That's enough. Don't you remember Sri Ramakrishna's song?"

Narendra sang :

O S'yāmā, my only hope is in Thy hallowed name!
What need have I of kos'ā and kus'ī?[12] What need of
    smiles and conventions?
Thy name dissolves death's bonds, as S'iva has proclaimed,
And I myself am S'iva's servant; whom else should I obey?
O Mother, come what may, I shall repeat Thy name;
Why should I fret myself to death? To S'iva's words I cling.

He sang again :

Mere babes are we, Father, with baby minds;
At every step we stumble and fall.
Why, then, must Thou show us Thy terrible face?
Why, Lord, must we ever behold Thy frown?

PRASANNA : " Now you are saying that there is a God. Again, it is you who say that according to Chārvāka and many other thinkers the world was self-created."

---

[12] Metal articles used in the temple worship.

NARENDRA: "Haven't you studied chemistry? Who combines the different elements? It is a human hand that combines hydrogen, oxygen, and electricity to prepare water. Everybody admits the existence of an intelligent Force—a Force that is the essence of knowledge and that guides all these phenomena."

PRASANNA: "How are we to know that God is kind?"

NARENDRA: "The Vedas say, 'That which is Thy compassionate face.' John Stuart Mill said the same thing. He said 'How much kindness must He have, who has implanted kindness in the hearts of men.' The Master used to say: 'Faith is the one essential thing. God exists. He is very near us. Through faith alone one sees Him.'

Narendra sang:

Where are you seeking Me, My servant? I am very close to you.
Far away you still are seeking, though I am so very near.
I am not in skin or hair, I am not in bones or flesh,
Not in mosque and not in temple, not in Kās'ī or Kailās.
Never will you come on Me in Ayodhyā or Dwārakā:
But you will be sure to find Me if you search where faith abides.
Not in pleasant tasks or yoga, not in vairāgya or sannyās,
Yet I come without delaying if you only search for Me.

PRASANNA: "Sometimes you say that God does not exist, and now you are saying all these things! You are not consistent. You keep changing your opinions."

All laughed.

NARENDRA: "All right! I shall never change what I have just said. As long as one has desires and cravings, so long one doubts the existence of God. A man cherishes some desire or other. Perhaps he has the desire to study or pass the university examination or become a scholar and so forth and so on."

Narendra sang again, in a voice choked with emotion:

Hail, to Thee, our God and Lord! Hail, giver of every
blessing!
Hail, Thou giver of good!
O Redeemer from fear, from danger and suffering!
Upholder of the worlds!
Hail, Lord! Victory to Thee!

Unfathomable and infinite, immeasurable, beyond compare,
O God, none equals Thee!
Lord of the Universe! O all-pervading Truth!
Thou the Ātman supreme!
Hail, Lord! Victory to Thee!

O Thou, the all-compassionate One, adored by the whole
universe,
I bow before Thy feet!
Thou art the only refuge in life and death, O Lord;
Before Thy feet I bow!
Hail, Lord! victory to Thee!

This is our only prayer, O Lord! O What other boon can we
implore?
Thus do we pray to Thee:
Grant us true wisdom here, and in the life hereafter
Reveal Thyself to us.
Hail, Lord! Victory to Thee!

Again Narendra sang, describing how very near God is to us—as near as the musk to the deer—and exhorting his brother disciples to drink deep from the cup of divine Bliss :

Drinking the bliss of Hari from the cup of prema.
Sādhu, be intoxicated !
Childhood you spent in crying and youth in women's control ;
Now, in your old age, full of phlegm and wind,
You wait for the funeral couch to bear you to the cremation
    ground.

Within the musk-deer's navel the fragrant musk is found ;
But how can you make it understand ?
Without the proper teacher to guide him on his way,
Man, too, is blindly roaming through the world,
Deluded as the foolish deer that wanders round and round
    the woods.

M. heard all this from the verandah.

Narendra got up. As he left the room he remarked, " My brain is heated by talking to these youngsters."

He met M. on the verandah and said, " Please, let us have a drink of water."

One of the members of the math said to Narendra, "Why, then, do you say that God does not exist ?"

Narendra laughed.

Monday, May 9, 1887

The next morning M. was sitting alone under a tree in the garden. He said to himself: " Sri Ramakrishna has made the brothers of the monastery renounce 'woman and gold'. Ah, how eager they are to realize God ! This place has become a veritable

Vaikuntha and the brothers living here are embodiments of Nārāyana. It is not many days since the Master passed away! that is why all the ideas and ideals he stood for are there, almost intact. 'The same Ayodhyā—only Rama is not there.' The Master has made these brothers renounce their homes. Why has he kept a few in the world? Is there no way of liberation for them?"

From a room upstairs Narendra saw M. sitting alone under the tree. He came down and said with a smile, "Hello, M.; What are you doing?"

After a little conversation M. said to him: "Ah, you have such a sweet voice. Please sing a hymn."

Narendra sang the following hymn to Śiva, in which the devotee prays for forgiveness for his sins:

> Even before I saw the light of this world, my sins from previous births,
>
> Through which I passed because of desire for the fruit of my deeds,
>
> Punished me as I lay in my mother's womb.
>
> There I was boiled in the midst of filthy things;
>
> Who can describe the pain that afflicts the child in its Mother's womb?
>
> Therefore, O Śiva! O Mahādeva! O Śambhu! forgive me, I pray, for my transgressions.
>
> In childhood my suffering never came to an end;
>
> My body was covered with filth and I craved for my mother's breasts.
>
> Over my body and limbs I had no control;

I was pursued by troublesome flies and mosquitoes;

Day and night I cried with the pain of many an ailment, foregetting Thee, O S'ankara!

Therefore, O S'iva! O Mahādeva! O S'ambhu! forgive me, I pray, for my transgressions.

In youth the venomous snakes of sound, sight, taste, touch and smell,

Bit into my vitals and slew my discrimination;

I was engrossed in the pleasures of wealth, sons and a youthful wife.

Alas! my heart, bereft of the thought of S'iva,
Was filled with arrogance and pride.

Therefore, O S'iva! O Mahādeva! O S'ambhu! forgive me, I pray, for my transgressions.

Now in old age my senses have lost the power of proper judging and acting;

My body, though still not wholly bereft of life,

Is weak and senile from many afflictions, from sins and illnesses and bereavements;

But even now my mind, instead of meditating on S'iva,

Runs after vain desires and hollow delusions.

Therefore, O S'iva! O Mahādeva! O S'ambhu! forgive me, I pray, for my transgressions.

The duties laid down in the smriti—perilous and abstruse— are now beyond me;

How can I speak of the Vedic injunctions for brāhmins, as means for attaining Brahman?

Never yet have I rightly grasped, through discrimination,

The meaning of hearing the scriptures from the guru and
reasoning on his instruction;

How then can I speak of reflecting on truth without
interruption?

Therefore, O S'iva! O Mahādeva! O S'ambhu! forgive me,
I pray, for my transgressions.

Not even once have I finished my bath before sunrise and
brought from the Ganges

Water to bathe Thy holy image;

Never, from the deep woods, have I brought the sacred
vilva leaves for Thy worship;

Nor have I gathered full-blown lotuses from the lakes,

Nor ever arranged the lights and the incense for worshipping
Thee.

Therefore, O S'iva! O Mahādeva! O S'ambhu! forgive me,
I pray, for my transgressions.

I have not bathed Thine image with milk and honey, with
butter and other oblations;

I have not decked it with fragrant sandal-paste;

I have not worshipped Thee with golden flowers, with
incense, with camphor-flame and savoury offerings.

Therefore, O S'iva! O Mahādeva! O S'ambhu! forgive me,
I pray, for my transgressions.

I have not made rich gifts to the brāhmins cherishing in my
heart,

O Mahādeva, Thy sacred form:

I have not made in the sacred fire the million oblations of
butter,

Repeating the holy mantra given to me by my guru;

Never have I done penance along the Gānges with japa and study of the Vedas.

Therefore. O S'iva! O Mahādeva! O S'ambhu! forgive me, I pray, for my transgressions.

I have not sat in the lotus posture, nor have I ever controlled
The prāna along the Sushumnā, repeating the syllable Om;
Never have I suppressed the turbulent waves of my mind, nor merged the self-effulgent Om

In the ever shining Witness-Consciousness, whose nature is that of the highest Brahman;

Nor have I, in samādhi, meditated on S'ankara, who dwells in every form as the inner Guide.

Therefore, O S'iva! O Mahādeva! O S'ambhu! forgive me, I pray, for my transgressions.

Never, O S'iva! have I seen Thee, the Pure, the Unattached, the naked One,

Beyond the three gunas, free from delusion and darkness, absorbed in meditation,

And ever aware of the true nature of the world;

Nor, with a longing heart, have I meditated on Thine auspicious and sin-destroying form.

Therefore. O S'iva! O Mahādeva! O S'ambhu! forgive me, I pray, for my transgressions.

O mind, to gain liberation, concentrate wholly on S'iva,
The sole Reality underlying the worlds, the Giver of good;
Whose head is illumined by the crescent moon and in whose hair the Ganges is hidden;

Whose fire-darting eyes consumed the god of earthly love; whose throat and ears are decked with snakes;

Whose upper garment is a comely elephant-skin.

Of what avail are all the other rituals?

O mind, of what avail are wealth or horses, elephants or a kingdom?

Of what avail the body or a house?

Know all these to be but momentary and quickly shun them;

Worship S'iva, as your guru instructs you, for the attaining of Self-knowledge.'

Day by day does man come nearer to death;

His youth wears away; the day that is gone never returns.

Almighty Time devours everything;

Fickle as lightning is the goddess of fortune.

O S'iva! O Giver of shelter to those that come to Thee for refuge!

Protect me, who have taken refuge at Thy feet.

I salute the ever auspicious S'iva, the home of peace,

Who sits in the lotus posture; who has five mouths and three eyes;

Who holds in both His hands weapons and gong and drum;

Who is bedecked with many an ornament;

Whose skin is clear as crystal; who is Pārvatī's Lord.

I salute the self-effulgent Guru of the gods, the Lord of Umā;

I salute the cause of the universe;

I salute the Lord of beasts, adorned with snakes;

I salute S'iva, whose three eyes shine like the sun, the moon and fiire ;

I salute the Beloved of Krishna; I salute S'ankara, who bestows boons on His devotees and gives them shelter; I salute the auspicious S'iva.

O S'iva! white is Thy body, covered with ashes ; white shine Thy teeth when Thou smilest !

White is the skull Thou holdest in Thy hand; white is Thy club, which threatens the wicked !

White is the bull on which Thou ridest; white are the rings that hang from Thine ears !

White appear Thy matted locks, covered with the form of the Gānges ;

White shines the moon on Thy forehead !

May He who is all white, all pure, bestow on me the treasure of forgiveness for my transgressions !

O S'iva, forgive all the sins that I have committed

With hands or feet, with words or body, with ears or eyes, with mind or heart ;

Forgive my sins, those past and those that are yet to come !

Victory unto S'iva, the ocean of compassion, the great God, the abode of blessedness !

After the hymn Narendra and M. talked again.

NARENDRA : " You may speak of leading a detached life in the world and all that, but you will not attain anything unless you renounce ' woman and gold '. Don't you feel disgusted with your wife's body ?

Fools enjoy the contact of the body, filled with filth, peopled with worms, foul of smell by nature, made of flesh, blood, bone and marrow; but the wise shun it.

"Vain is the life of a person who does not take delight in the teachings of Vedānta and drink the nectar of divine Bliss. Listen to a song."

Narendra sang:

O man, abandon your delusion! Cast aside your wicked
    counsels !
Know the Lord and free yourself from earthly suffering !
For a few days' pleasure only, you have quite forgotten Him
Who is the comrade of your soul. Alas, what mockery !

"No liberation is possible for a man unless he puts on the loin-cloth of a sannyāsī. The world must be renounced."

Narendra sang from the Five Stanzas on the glory of the monk's loin-cloth:

Roaming ever in the grove of Vedānta,
Ever pleased with his beggar's morsel
Ever walking with heart free from sorrow,
Blest indeed is the wearer of the loin-cloth......

Continuing, Narendra said: "Why should a man be entangled in worldliness ? Why should he be ensnared by māyā ? What is man's real nature ? He is the blessed S'iva, the embodiment of Bliss and Spirit."

He sang S'ankarāchārya's Six Stanzas on Nirvāna;

Om, I am neither mind, intelligence, ego, nor chitta,
Neither ears nor tongue nor the senses of smell and sight ;
Nor am I ether, earth, fire, water, or air :
I am pure Knowledge and Bliss : I am S'iva ! I am S'iva !

Narendra recited another hymn, the Eight Stanzas on the glory of Krishna:

I am consumed with false desires and wrapped in the sleep of lust :

> Save me, O Madhusūdana !
> Thou art my only Refuge, Lord ! I have no other salvation.
> I am entrapped in the mire of sin :
> O Madhusūdana, redeem me !

> I am ensnared in the net of love for children, wife and home :
> Save me, O Madhūsudana !
> I am without devotion, helpless, smitten by wrong desire,
> Afflicted with grief and misery :
> O Madhusūdana, redeem me !

> Lord, I have neither master nor place of shelter to call my
> own :
> Save me, O Madhusūdana !
> Utterly wearied out am I by all this going and coming
> Along the endless road of life :
> O Madhusūdana, redeem me !

> From this hard and unavailing journey through life and death,
> Save me, O Madhusūdana !
> Many the births that I have seen in many a bodily form,
> And painful it is in the mother's womb :
> O Madhusūdana, redeem me !

> To Thee I come for salvation out of the cycle of existence :
> Save me, O Madhūsudana !
> For I am terrified alike of old age and of death :
> I come to Thee for shelter, Lord !
> O Madhusūdana, redeem me !

> Never a good deed have I done, but many have been my sins :
> Save me, O Madhusūdana !

Headlong have I fallen into the mire of worldliness ;
Countless the births I have endured :
O Madhusūdana, redeem me !

I have lorded it over men, but happiness is not there :
Save me, O Madhusūdana !
What my words have promised, my deeds have never carried
    out ;
Lord, I am full of wretchedness :
O Madhusūdana, redeem me !

If as a man or a woman I must be born again and again—
Save me, O Madhusūdana !—
May my devotion be unswerving to Thy feet, O Lord !
From the delusion of this world,
O Madhusūdana, redeem me !

M. remained spell bound as he listened to these hymns sung
by Narendra. He said to himself : " How intense Narendra's
dispassion is ! This is how he has infused the spirit of dispassion
into the hearts of the other brothers of the monastery. The
very contact with them awakens in the hearts of the Master's
householder devotees the desire for renunciation of ' woman and
gold '. Ah, how blessed are these all-renouncing brothers ! Why
has the Master kept us few in the world ? Will he show us a
way ? Will he give us the spirit of renunciation, or will he delude
us with worldliness ? "

After the meal all were resting. The elder Gopāl was
copying some songs. Niranjan was on a visit to his mother.
S'arat, Bāburām, and Kālī were in Purī.

Narendra, with one or two brothers, left for Calcutta. He
had to see to his lawsuit. He was going to return in the
evening ; the brothers could not bear his absence,

In the afternoon Rabindra arrived, looking like a mad person. He was barefoot and had only half of his black-bordered cloth round his waist. His eyeballs were rolling like a madman's. All asked him anxiously what was the matter.

"Let me recover my breath!" he said. "I shall tell you everything presently. I am certainly not going back home; I shall stay at this very place with you all. She is certainly a traitor! Let me tell you something, friends. For her sake I gave up my habit of drinking, which I had indulged for five years. I have not taken a drop for the last eight months. And she is a traitor!"

The brothers of the math said: "Be calm, please! How did you come?"

RABINDRA: "I have come barefoot all the way from Calcutta."

The brothers asked him where he had lost the other half of his cloth.

RABINDRA: "When I was leaving her place she began to pull at my cloth. That is how half of it was torn off."

The brothers told him to bathe in the Ganges and cool off; then they would hear his story.

Rabindra belonged to a respectable kāyastha family of Calcutta. He was twenty or twenty-two years old. He had first met Sri Ramakrishna at the Dakshineswar temple and had received his special blessing. On one occasion he had spent three nights with the Master. His disposition was very sweet and tender and the Master had loved him dearly. Once he had said to Rabindra: "You will have to wait some time; you have to go through a few more experiences. Nothing can be done now. You see, the police can't do much just when the robbers attack a house. When the plundering is almost over, the police make their arrests."

Rabindra had many virtues. He was devoted to God and to service of the poor. He had many spiritual qualities. But he had walked into the snare of a prostitute. Now, suddenly, he had discovered that the woman was being unfaithful to him. Therefore he had come to the math in this dishevelled state, resolved not to go back to the world.

A devotee accompanied Rabindra to the Ganges. It was his inmost desire that Rabindra's spiritual consciousness should be awakened in the company of these holy men. When Rabindra finished his bath, the devotee took him to the adjacent cremation ground, showed him the corpses lying about, and said : " The brothers of the math come here every now and then to meditate on God. It is a good place for meditation. Here one sees clearly that the world is impermanent. "

Rabindra sat down in the cremation ground to meditate. But he could not meditate long ; his mind was restless.

Rabindra and the devotee returned to the math. They went to the worship room to salute the Deity. The devotee said to him, " The brothers of the math meditate in this room. "

Rabindra sat there to meditate, but could not meditate long there either.

DEVOTEE : " How do you feel ? Is your mind very restless ? Is that why you have got up from your seat ? Perhaps you could not concentrate well "

RABINDRA : " I am sure I shall not go back to the world. But the mind is restless. "

M. and Rabindra were talking. No one else was present. M. was telling him stories from the life of Buddha. At that time the members of the math regularly read the lives of Buddha and Chaitanya. M. said to Rabindra that Buddha's spiritual consciousness was first awakened by hearing a song of some heavenly maidens.

M. sang the song:

> We moan for rest, alas! but rest can never find;
> We know not whence we come, nor where we float away.
> Time and again we tread this round of smiles and tears;
> In vain we pine to know whither our pathway leads,
> And why we play this empty play......

That night Narendra, Tārak and Harish returned from Calcutta. They said, "Oh, what a big meal we had!" They had been entertained by a devotee in Calcutta.

The members of the monastery assembled in the room of the "dānās". Narendra heard Rabindra's story. He sang by way of giving instruction to him:

> O man, abandon your delusion! Cast aside your wicked
>   counsels!
> Know the Lord and free yourself from earthly suffering!
> For a few days' pleasure only, you have quite forgotten Him
> Who is the Comrade of your soul. Alas, what mockery!

Narendra sang again:

> Drinking the Bliss of Hari from the cup of prema,
> Sādhu, be intoxicated!......

A few minutes later the brothers went to Kālī Tapasvī's room. Girish Ghosh had just sent two of his new books to the monastery: the *Life of Buddha* and the *Life of Chaitanya*.

Since the founding of the new math S'ashī had devoted himself heart and soul to the worship and service of the Master. All were amazed at his devotion. Just as he had tended Sri Ramakrishna's physical body during his illness, so now, with the same unswerving zeal, he worshipped the Master in the shrine room.

A member of the monastery was reading aloud from the lives of Buddha and Chaitanya. He was a little sarcastic while reading Chaitanya's life. Narendra snatched the book from his hand and said, " That is how you spoil a good thing !"

Narendra read the chapter describing how Chaitanya gave his love to all, from the brāhmin to the pariah.

A BROTHER : "I say that one person cannot give love to another person."

NARENDRA : " But the Master gave it to me."

BROTHER : " Well, are you sure, you have it ?"

NARENDRA : " What can you understand about love ? You belong to the servant class. All of you must serve me and massage my feet. Don't flatter yourselves by thinking you have understood everything. Now go and prepare a smoke for me.

All laughed.

THE BROTHER : "I surely will not."

M . (to himself) : " Sri Ramakrishna has transmitted mettle to all the brothers of the math. It is no monopoly of Narendra's. Is it possible to renounce 'woman and gold' without this inner fire ?"

May 10, 1887

It was Tuesday, a very auspicious day for the worship of the divine Mother. Arrangement were being made for Her special worship at the monastery.

M. was going to the Ganges to take his bath. Rabindra was walking alone on the roof. He heard Narendra singing the Six Stanzas on Nirvāna :

> Death or fear I have none, nor any distinction of caste ;
> Neither father nor mother nor even a birth have I ;
> Neither friend nor comrade, neither disciple nor guru ;
> I am pure Knowledge and Bliss: I am S'iva ! I am S'iva !
>
> I have no form or fancy; the All-pervading am I ;
> Everywhere I exist, yet I am beyond the senses ;
> Neither salvation am I, nor anything that may be known ;
> I am pure Knowledge and Bliss : I am S'iva ! I am S'iva !

Rabindra went to the Ganges to take his bath. Presently he returned to the monastery clad in his wet cloth.

Narendra said to M. in a whisper : " He has bathed in the Ganges. It would be good to initiate him now into sannyās."

Both Narendra and M. smiled.

Prasanna asked Rabindra to change his wet cloth and gave him a dry gerruā cloth. Narendra said to M. " Now he is going to put on the cloth of renunciation."

M. *(with a smile)* : " What kind of renunciation ?"

NARENDRA : " Why, the renunciation of 'woman and gold.' "

Rabindra put on the ochre cloth and entered Kālī Tapasvī's room to meditate.